THE DYNAMIC INTROVERT

LEADING
QUIETLY
WITH
PASSION
AND
PURPOSE

LESLEY
TAYLOR

Copyright ©2015 by Lesley Taylor

All rights reserved. No part of this book may be reproduced (except in cases of brief excerpts used in book reviews or critical articles) or transmitted in any form or by any means, electronic or mechanical, including photocopying, recording, or any information storage and retrieval system, even if for educational or non-profit purposes, without permission in writing from the publisher, Western Winds Publishing, Inc.

Published by Western Winds Publishing, Inc.
186-8120 No 2 Road
Richmond, B.C.
V7C 5J8
ISBN # 978-0-9936546-2-6

Second Edition, 2015
Author: Lesley Taylor
www.thedynamicintrovert.com

Editor: Margaret Davidson

Book Cover Design: SpicaBookDesign
Typeset in *Berling* with *Baker* display at SpicaBookDesign

Printed in Canada
by Printorium Bookworks/Island Blue, Victoria B.C.

Acknowledgements

Many people have played a role in bringing this book to fruition and helping me realize my lifelong goal of becoming a writer. Special thanks to Mike Johnson who opened my eyes to the challenges and opportunities faced by introverts. As I learned about introverts and introversion I discovered a great many surprising things about myself that I would not have learned if I had not delved deeply into this subject.

I would like to thank Margaret Davidson for editing the manuscript and for keeping me on track with her positive comments and thoughtful suggestions for improvements. In particular I am indebted to Margaret for suggesting the title The Dynamic Introvert.

Many of the comments and stories in the book come from dynamic introverts who participated in my on-line survey. Your stories make the book come alive and I thank-you from the bottom of my heart. Thanks also to all of you who sent me articles, links, blog posts and information about introverts and introversion.

Writing is a challenging endeavour and I could not have completed this project without the ongoing support of my community of cheerleaders: Norma Campbell, Barry and Luke MacKinnon, Debbie Lindsey, Nora Wright, Denise Sketches, Lois Thomson, Bruce Stewart, Cathy MacKay, Marley Holowach, Peter Andersen, Dave Dalley, Karen Edwards, Sheila MacCallum, Ann Vanderbijl, Cindy Johal,

Lily Pollard, Ariba Dahl, Shirley Nelson, Ken Ostoich, Chris Norman, Cheryl Jeffs and Susan Einarsson.

Finally, I would like to dedicate this book to all of the introverts who quietly make the world a better place.

Preface

The idea for this book evolved from a conversation with a fellow introvert. That initial conversation left me yearning for more knowledge and understanding as to what it means to be an introvert in the 21st century. I hope that the book will spark a similar reaction in you.

Although I've been an introvert all of my life I had not given much thought to this aspect of my personality until early in 2012. In the course of researching and writing The Dynamic Introvert I discovered that I was not alone, that in fact, many people do not give much thought to whether they are introverted or extroverted. This may not be a challenge for extroverts as much of the world seems to be designed with them in mind. But—as I suggest throughout the book—introverts need to become more aware and conscious of their introversion. As with many things in life, introversion can be a "double edged sword". Our personality can result in challenges, especially if we aspire to be leaders, but it will also give us the edge that we need in order to succeed in our rapidly changing world.

I hope you will find this book a valuable reference and I would like to hear from you as to how you've put the ideas into practice.

I encourage you to visit the website www.thedynamicintrovert.com where you will find additional resources and an invitation to become part of a growing community of dynamic introverts who are providing extraordinary leadership around the world.

>Lesley Taylor
>Richmond, B.C.
>info@thedynamicintrovert.com
>August 10, 2015

Author's Note

The terms introversion and extraversion are credited to Swiss psychiatrist Carl Jung. For the purpose of this book I will be using the layperson's spelling of introvert and extrovert unless I use a direct quote that includes an alternate spelling in it. As introversion and extroversion exist on a continuum, most people's personalities fall somewhere between the two. The word ambivert describes someone whose personality is a balance of both introversion and extroversion.

You may notice that I don't use the term introvertism. It is sometimes used interchangeably with introversion but it is not as popular. A recent Google search showed over one million results for the word introversion and only 10,900 results for the word introvertism.

There are numerous definitions of introversion and many of them describe introverts in a narrow way. A common misperception is that an introvert is a shy, reticent, and typically self-centered person. Many introverts find this characterization to be negative and not representative of how they see themselves. In my research I discovered that introverts describe themselves in many different ways and refuse to be limited by the more traditional definitions.

I recognize that there is much more to our personalities than just the introversion and extroversion continuum but it is beyond the scope of this book to go into detail about the range of personality types. There are many excellent resources available in print and online for readers who want to learn more about their personalities.

Introduction

> "I THINK MANY OF US ARE DYNAMIC.
> WE JUST MAKE LESS FUSS AND NOISE ABOUT BEING DYNAMIC
> THAN SOME EXTRAVERTS. OUR ENERGY AND ENTHUSIASM IS
> OFTEN HIDDEN FROM THE EXTERNAL WORLD."
> Dr. Judy Curson[1]

What is a dynamic introvert? Is a dynamic introvert an oxymoron, two words that seemingly contradict one another (think jumbo shrimp) or can introverts really be dynamic?

As I began to explore what it meant to be an introvert I discovered that introverts identify themselves in surprisingly different ways. There are self-described social introverts, extroverted introverts, quiet introverts, conscious introverts, fearless introverts and accessible introverts.

In contrast, a quick look at the thesaurus suggests that introverts are cool, collected, introspective, bashful, withdrawn, and solitary. More often than not it is these words that we associate with introverted behaviour. I also believe that we see what we want or expect to see so it is no wonder that we only see the quiet, reserved introverts in our lives. We tend to overlook the more dynamic introverts among us, perhaps believing that the more social of us are really extroverts and not introverts at all.

My leadership journey began many years ago. As a child I loved building forts in our basement and in the rafters of the car port. I also loved exploring on my own. For a time when I was 8 years old we lived in a rural area and I would disappear for hours by myself. We had farmland and a peat bog behind us and the Fraser River across the road in front of our house so I had lots of places to investigate. One of my favourite memories involves spending time on my own quietly exploring the peat bog in winter. The land between the farm I lived on and the bog was populated with large evergreen trees and when it snowed I would spend hours staying dry under the trees hidden away from the world.

Looking back I realize that I was fearless in my solo explorations but my courage vanished once I was in school. You see I was terrified of being called upon by my teachers to answer questions in front of other students. At that age, I had no idea that I was an introvert.

As I got older I looked forward to attending university but when I arrived there I struggled with having to give presentations and ended up choosing classes in which I could avoid speaking in front of my peers. It wasn't until I had graduated and started working as a professional social worker that it finally dawned on me that my fear of being the centre of attention was affecting my ability to advance my career.

As a first step I decided that I needed to overcome my fear of public speaking. In my workplace, social workers and psychologists met monthly to discuss journal articles or share cases. I was impressed by the ease with which some of my colleagues could stand in front of the group and present and I vowed to myself that one day I would be able to do that too.

Despite being uncomfortable in the spotlight, I took every opportunity I could to practise public speaking. That was thirty years ago and today I am comfortable and at ease speaking in front of a group when I have had time to prepare, although my preference at heart is to sit back and observe.

Of course being able to speak to a group is only one of the skills required of leaders in today's rapidly changing society. Most workplaces demand skills outside the comfort zone of many introverts: working in and leading teams, networking, self-promotion, working quickly or multi-tasking, and dealing with conflict, to name a few. As you will discover in this book, these are all skills that can be learned. And when we are engaged in something that we feel passionate about, it is easier to excel in areas in which we would normally not feel at ease.

I discovered this many times as my career progressed. My passion for what I was doing enabled me to move into informal leadership roles that I otherwise would have avoided. These informal roles were important stepping stones to a number of exciting opportunities that were presented to me as I moved forward in my career.

If you are not already in a leadership position, you can still step up and lead. I am talking about the difference between formal and informal leadership here. Formal leadership roles are the ones that are typically recognized through job descriptions, salary, status, and position in an organization's hierarchy. The chief executive officer or CEO, executive director, vice president, board member and management positions are examples but there will be others depending on the organization and the industry in which you work.

In contrast, informal leadership is leadership that may not be officially sanctioned but is still very important to an organization's success. To be an effective informal leader you need to be respected by the people with whom you work and able to use your personal influence to engage them.

And as I learned from my own experience there are different ways that we can provide informal leadership.

When organizations are in flux there is always work that needs to be done. For whatever reason, these important roles go unfulfilled. At university I discovered that I have a passion for community and organizational development but as a clinical social worker this type of work was not part of my job description and so was out of reach. I overcame this obstacle by volunteering with various community agencies where I was able to develop my leadership skills.

It didn't take long before the opportunity arose for me to showcase these skills in my workplace. At the time I was working in a small urban hospital. It was a period of rapid change but the hospital did not have the resources to support an organizational development department and so I offered to lead team building retreats for my own department and then strategic planning sessions for other departments. Despite the fact that these initiatives were not in my job description, people noticed the leadership that I was providing and this recognition led to future career opportunities. I will share some of these experiences in later chapters.

Despite being encouraged to take on formal leadership roles I never considered how being an introvert factored into the leadership equation. That awareness came years later when one of my managers expressed the opinion that, because I am an introvert, I would never be a good leader. I also didn't realize that my boss was not alone in thinking that extroverts make better leaders than introverts.

At the time I didn't pay much attention to what he had said, but his words must have resonated because I found myself reflecting on them while conducting research for The Dynamic Introvert. The idea of writing about introversion and leadership had not occurred to me until I was introduced to the topic in 2012 by Mike Johnson, a student in one of my leadership courses. Mike urged me to read Jennifer Kahnweiler's book The Introverted Leader[2] and it was at that point that I realized that introverted people do, in fact, make excellent leaders.

My purpose in writing this book is to help you reframe the way you think about yourself as an introvert and as a leader. As an introvert you no longer have to hide your true self or pretend to be an extrovert in order to get ahead in the world. As a dynamic introvert you can be a force for positive change by building on your quiet strengths.

Throughout this book I have shared my own stories in addition to those of friends and colleagues. I have changed the names of some of the people involved in order to preserve their privacy. I have also included quotes from 50 self-described introverts who participated in a leadership and introversion survey that I conducted in 2012.

This online survey provided a rich source of data, and quotes from the participants illustrate the ideas I put forward in this book. I also collected information about introversion from other sources, including a focus group and one-to-one interviews with a diverse group of introverts whom I know both personally and professionally.

I am deeply grateful for the information that I received from experts such as Adam Grant, Ralph Kilman, Stacey Doepner-Hove, Denise Buchanan, Ann Vanderbijl, Rosalie Boulter, Barbara Hughes, and Judy Curson who responded to my questions by sharing their knowledge and providing additional resources and suggestions.

I would also like to acknowledge the many organizations that have given me permission to link to their websites. You will find a list of these resources in the Notes section of this book.

Table of Contents

PREFACE v
AUTHOR'S NOTE. vii
INTRODUCTION ix

1   INTROVERTS ARE QUIET LEADERS 1
      What Makes a Successful Leader? 4
      Why Extroverts Succeed 5
      It Takes Courage to Lead 7
      The Introverted Brand 8
      Self-awareness, Self-management & Reflection 9
      Rethinking the Way We look at Introverts 9
      It's Time for a Sea Change 11
      Chapter Summary 12

2   THE POWER OF INTROVERTED LEADERS. 13
      Reflecting on the Six R's. 15
          Role Models. 15
          Recognition 17
          Resources. 18
          Respect 19
          Resilience. 21
          Respite. 22
      The Challenges of Leadership. 23
          Being SELF-AWARE. 23
          What IS Your Vision? 24
          Questioning the Process 25
          Engaging Others 26
          Providing Encouragement 27

    Leadership Challenges for Introverts 29
    Finding Our Voice 32
    Stereotypes and Myths about Leadership. 35
    Level Five Leadership. 35
    Understanding Power and Influence. 36
    Conflict. 38
    Leadership, Reflection & Learning 40
    What challenges do introverts face in the workplace? 40
    Learning Organizations 41
    Listen and speak without judgement 42
    How has being an introvert affected your career?. 43
    Self-Leadership & Personal Mastery. 43
    Chapter Summary 44

3   THE ENERGY EQUATION 45
    Different Types of Energy. 47
    Try this Exercise. 50
    Alone Time. 51
    Leaders Need Abundant Energy. 52
    Organizational Energy 54
    Creating Your Ideal Environment. 58
    The Importance of Knowing Your Life Purpose. 60
    Avoiding Burnout 62
    Unfairness. 64
    Emotional Intelligence, Introversion and Burnout 64
    Take Action to Avoid Burnout 66
    Chapter Summary 68

4   PERSONAL BRANDING & SELF PROMOTION FOR INTROVERTS 69
    Asking for Feedback 72
    Your Brand is Your Reputation. 74
    Be Intentional About Your Presence. 76
    Charisma 77
    Networking. 78

Mentors and Coaches 81
Get over Your Fear of Success............................82
Chapter Summary 83

5   THE INTROVERTED LEADER ADVANTAGE 84
    Leading Engaged Employees............................86
    Respecting a Variety of Communication Styles 87
    The Invisible Majority – Supporting a Broader
    Definition of Diversity 88
    Awareness and Education Are Key...................... 89
    Mindsets...92
    The Role of Human Resources 94
        The Recruiting Process 94
        The Onboarding Process 97
        Performance Reviews..............................97
        Encouraging Introverts to Do Their Best Work.......... 99
        Mentoring and Coaching..........................103
    The Hidden Costs of Ignoring Introverts 105
    What can organizations do to address this issue? 106
    Chapter Summary 106

6   YOUR PERSONAL LEADERSHIP DEVELOPMENT PLAN 108
    What is a Personal Leadership Development Plan? 110
        Purpose 111
        Developing Our Personalities 113
        Values 115
    Strengths and Areas for Improvement 116
    Goal Setting & Action Plans...........................117
    Self-awareness......................................119
    Authenticity 120
    Journaling...121
    Your Legacy 123
    Chapter Summary 124

7   THE QUIET REVOLUTION HAS BEGUN................125
    A Perfect Storm 127
    A Call to Action 131
    Building Community 133
    Chapter Summary 136

AFTERWORD..137
NOTES..142
INDEX..153
ABOUT THE AUTHOR 159

CHAPTER ONE
Introverts are Quiet Leaders

"TO BE DYNAMIC IS TO BE EVER CHANGING,
EVER GROWING, EVER DEVELOPING."
James B. Pratt. Jr.[1]

Recently I found myself scanning local job postings to see which qualities organizations were looking for in their prospective leaders. I was surprised by the number of advertisements that included the word dynamic in them. I also noticed that the search for dynamic workers was not limited to the ranks of leaders. A local storage company has been running an ad on the radio with the aim of finding dynamic employees. But what exactly are they looking for? What does it mean to be dynamic?

One of my favorite definitions is from self-described introvert and blogger James B. Pratt Jr. The qualities that Mr. Pratt describes at the beginning of this chapter can apply to both introverts and extroverts alike. Adjectives such as positive, full of energy and brimming with new ideas also describe those of us who are dynamic. But extroverts are more likely to express their dynamic natures openly, while introverts, as described by Dr. Judy Curan in the introduction to this book, "hide their energy and enthusiasm from the external world".

This is unfortunate because employers looking for dynamic leaders are more likely to search for individuals who are outwardly positive, extroverted, charming, and energetic. They are not looking for people who are quiet and reflective. Perhaps it is time to rethink or reframe how we want our leaders to behave. What are the most important qualities for leaders in the 21st century? These are questions being asked by Human Resource experts across the globe as they scramble to prepare the next generation of leaders.

In 2008, the Chartered Institute of Personnel & Development (CIPD) proclaimed, "There is a looming leadership crisis in the West." This attention-getting quote refers to the leadership crisis that is predicted to occur when managers and leaders from the baby boom generation retire. In the document "Engaging Leadership"[2] the CIPD sounds the alarm that the "shrinking talent pool from which future leaders will be drawn is diminishing."

One of the assumptions in *The Dynamic Introvert* is that introverts make up a large part of this "shrinking talent pool" and yet their leadership potential often goes unnoticed. I believe that the "pool" is actually larger than people originally thought and—given the opportunity—introverts will step in and fill the looming leadership gap.

In order for this to happen though, organizations must recognize that introverts already make up a sizable portion of their workforce despite the incorrect assumption that introverts are in the minority.

In 2002, when Marty Olsen Laney wrote the bestseller *The Introvert Advantage*,[3] it was believed that only one-third of the general population had introverted tendencies. We now know that introverts make up as much as one-half of the population.[4] Despite this fact, "extraverts are more likely to be chosen for leadership positions".[5]

As I began my search for answers to this conundrum, I came across a leadership website[6] for introverts. In 2009, Dr. Judy Curson, one of the site's originators, was inspired to take action when she read the following passage in her son's physical education textbook:

People can be divided into two identified types:[7]

- Introverts—these are people who are quiet and self-centered, not high in confidence, not looking to lead

- Extroverts—confident and outgoing people with high opinions of themselves, they tend to be leaders

Dr. Curson, who identifies herself as an introvert, was concerned that the above description was misleading and potentially damaging to the students who read the textbook. Her concerns led to her own search for information on introversion and leadership. With the help of colleague Cassy Taylor, Dr. Curson was able to secure funding from the South Central Strategic Health Authority and the Welsh government to develop the leadership website. The site, which is a valuable source of information for both introverts and those wanting to "coach, support, manage, and work with them" has been well received and is being used as a resource for post graduate medical education in the U.K[8]

WHAT MAKES A SUCCESSFUL LEADER?

Many of the misconceptions about introversion and leadership may reflect the fact that there is considerable confusion about leadership in general. A recent Google search using the word leadership turned up 639,000,000 responses and an Amazon search showed 148,751 books in the leadership category. But, as David Rock notes, "there are still huge gaps in our understanding of leadership."[9]

As far back as 1945,[10] researchers at Ohio State University began studying the behaviour of leaders in order to discover what differentiated successful leaders from unsuccessful ones. They found that there were no specific traits that could be attributed to outstanding leaders: some leaders were energetic and quick thinking, while others were quiet and modest.

More recently, James M. Kouzes and Barry Z. Posner wrote *The Leadership Challenge*, a practical leadership book based on over 25 years of research into what makes leaders great. Their research revealed that "leadership is an identifiable set of skills and abilities that are available to all of us."[11] In *The Dynamic Introvert*, I will explore some of the skills that introverts can develop in order to become effective leaders.

In 2009, a team of researchers led by Adam Grant[12] found that introverted leaders can be more effective than extroverted leaders in situations of rapid change especially when there is a need to engage everyone in the organization in finding innovative solutions to problems and new ways of doing business.

But the question still remains: if leadership is less about charisma and more about developing relationships and bringing out the best in people, why do we continue to believe so strongly that extroverts make the best leaders?

WHY EXTROVERTS SUCCEED

While evidence suggests that the preference for extroverts as leaders exists in all sectors of society, let's consider, as an example, one survey from the world of business. Nearly two-thirds of 1,542 senior managers surveyed in 2006 saw introversion as an impediment to reaching higher management levels.[13] Extroverts, it would seem, are deemed by virtue of their outgoing style to be more intelligent and therefore chosen for more leadership opportunities than are introverts, even though extroverts may not be the most appropriate leaders in every situation. More recently Adam McHugh wrote, "There may be no other feature of American life that contains as much bias toward extroversion as leadership."[14]

Thankfully, this widely held bias is being confronted. Daniel Quinn Mills who taught at the Harvard Business School for many years both acknowledges this bias and challenges its premise. "We perceive talkers as smarter than quiet types even though GPA (Grade Point Average) and SAT (college entry exam) and IQ test scores reveal this perception to be inaccurate."[15]

Jonathan Rauch, journalist and activist, writing in The Atlantic in 2003, makes the strong statement that introverts "are among the most misunderstood groups in America, possibly the world."[16] There are many reasons why this is the case and I will explore some of these in more detail in the chapters that follow.

My own perception is that introverts are misunderstood because we have had to pretend to be extroverts in order to succeed in life. Pretending begins early in life. From a young age many of us are encouraged by parents and teachers to be more extroverted in order to fit in at school. This expectation that introverts will do better in society as extroverts continues as we move from the classroom setting into the workplace.

In a world that values extroversion over introversion and leaders are expected to be persuasive, assertive, outgoing, and quick thinking, many introverts have had to suppress their natural tendencies.

What does this do to introverts who are not allowed to be true to themselves? There are often emotional consequences for the individual who must take on the persona of someone that he or she is not. As I point out in Chapter Three, this acting out of character can be stressful and potentially lead to burnout if it goes on too long.

Some introverts may actually prefer a level of anonymity. In my own experience I've always been more comfortable sharing the limelight than taking the credit for myself. However, I acknowledge that I feel a sense of satisfaction when people recognize my contributions and I have been fortunate, over the course of my career, to have had my leadership potential recognized by a number of senior leaders.

Jennifer Kahnweiler writes about turning a perceived weakness into a strength. "One well-respected manager was given feedback in his career that he was too low-key. In his future role as a senior leader he turned this laid-back persona into a presence. He had a strong ability to project a calm confidence—a sense of ease, poise, and self-assurance that transferred to all the people around him."[17]

I can relate to Kahnweiler's anecdote because I've been told that I have the ability to restore calm to a chaotic situation just by entering a room! We will delve into the importance of presence when we look at personal branding in Chapter Four.

"I have had six successful careers and become a leader in each one. My strengths are interest in people, communication skills, innovation, analysis, planning and follow through. All of these have benefited from my being an introvert, who thinks before he speaks, delivers on what he says, includes others in planning and builds trust." *Survey Participant*

IT TAKES COURAGE TO LEAD

Sir Winston Churchill once said, "Courage is what it takes to stand up and speak; courage is also what it takes to sit down and listen".[18] The late British prime minister was referring to the need for balance: sitting down and listening is as important as standing up and speaking. But, somehow our extroverted society has favoured speaking over listening. Introverts, who are more comfortable listening, are fully capable of providing leadership but as a necessary first step that they must find the courage to "stand up and speak."

Dr. Brené Brown, who teaches at the University of Houston, writes about vulnerability and leadership. She describes a courageous act as one that involves showing up and being seen.[19] This may not always be easy for introverts but crucial if we are assuming leadership roles in society.

Courage comes when we trust ourselves to know when it is the right time to speak up and when it is best to listen. From my perspective, gaining courage begins with knowing who we are and what we can contribute. We must be able to visualize how we want to show up in the world and what impact we want to have. We have to be honest with ourselves about our strengths and weaknesses and analyze what gets in the way of our becoming who we want to be. This self-confidence will provide a strong foundation from which to lead.

According to author Nancy Okerlund, the process of becoming more aware of who we are is powerful: she refers to this as "conscious introversion."[20] Of course Okerlund is referring to personal awareness in this quote but thanks to Susan Cain and other writers, there is a growing understanding in society about introversion in general.

THE INTROVERTED BRAND

Another reason that introverts might be overlooked is that we don't always realize we are capable of managing our personal brand or how important this is to our future success. We may inadvertently allow other people to make assumptions about us and this may not work in our favour, especially if we want to take on leadership roles. Promoting ourselves starts with an understanding of who we are: our personality, our interests, our skills and our values. It also means determining what success means to us.

Personal branding is not a new idea; in fact the term was coined by Tom Peters in a 1997 Fast Company article entitled "The Brand Called You."[21] As an introvert you need to take control of how you are perceived and brand yourself before someone else does. Do you want to be known as a meek, anti-social and ineffective leader? Or can you project yourself as a dynamic introvert who is quiet at times, creative, collaborative, and effective—a leader who listens to people and helps them do their best work?

Whatever your brand, it has to be authentic. We'll take a closer look in Chapter Three at the meaning of authenticity and how this contributes to becoming a dynamic introvert.

SELF-AWARENESS, SELF-MANAGEMENT & REFLECTION

Referring to the importance of developing our emotional intelligence, author Daniel Goleman states "From self-awareness—understanding one's emotions and being clear about one's purpose—flows self-management, the focused drive that all leaders need to achieve their goals."[22] Being emotionally intelligent and finding the time for introspection are now considered keys to leading a successful life and is increasingly expected in our leaders.

One advantage that introverts have over extroverts is our ability to stop and reflect on our experiences. It's not that extroverts can't and don't do this: it is just that introverts are hard wired to slow down, reflect and think before speaking. We know that introverts prefer quiet time and solitude in order to process the information that they are receiving. This time for reflection is necessary for learning and creativity and it improves decision-making.

Leadership expert Margaret Wheatly[23] challenges her readers to stop and reflect on the experiences that they are having and to make it possible for others to do the same. This may not be as challenging or difficult as we may think. As we become more comfortable voicing our own need for reflection, we can encourage others to follow our lead.

RETHINKING THE WAY WE LOOK AT INTROVERTS

What would happen if we reframed the way we look at introversion? What if we were to recognize and reward the positive elements of this personality trait? What if organizations were to realize the unique benefits that dynamic introverts provide?

First things first. We need to better understand the term introversion.

Until about a decade ago there was little understanding of introversion and few books published in the popular press. Introversion and shyness were often confused with each other. Even today you will find people using the words introversion and shyness interchangeably. But the two are not the same.

Shyness is a fear and avoidance of social situations. Unlike introverts who feel energized by spending time alone, shy people often want to connect with others but are afraid to do so. Both introverts and extroverts can be shy. The Shyness Research Institute[24] at Indiana University Southeast has a website with a number of tools and resources to help shy people understand and overcome their shyness.

There is, however, a close resemblance between introversion and sensitivity. In a Psychology Today blog post Elaine Aron explains that "both introverts and Highly Sensitive Persons (HSPs) reflect deeply, like meaningful conversations, and need lots of down time. Thus it is not surprising that 70% of HSPs are introverts. But that means 30% are extraverts."[25] Dr. Aron is the author of the best-selling book *The Highly Sensitive Person*.[26] You will find a self-test to help you determine how sensitive you are on her website.[27]

Much of the writing on introversion and leadership focuses on how introverts can become more extroverted or what professor Brian Little refers to as "pseudo extroversion".[28] As an introvert I acknowledge that we need to flex our extroverted selves from time to time, especially when we step into leadership positions. But we also need to recognize that as introverts we have our own strengths: qualities that are desperately needed in our loud, intrusive and demanding world.

In Chapter Two, we explore the strengths and the quiet power of introverted leaders. We will also review new research that demonstrates why introverts may make the best leaders in contemporary organizations. Chapter Three focuses on how we manage our personal energy: it is the one thing that readily differentiates introverts from extroverts. Chapter Four describes how personal branding is a key strategy for introverts wanting to excel and advance in their careers. In Chapter Five we delve into the main areas that organizations must focus on to successfully engage introverts. Chapter Six provides resources and information so that you can develop your own personal leadership development plan.

The final chapter explores why and how a more introverted society is gradually evolving and how dynamic introverts can lead this quiet revolution. Finally, I offer some thoughts for young introverts starting out in their careers.

Throughout the book I encourage you to **stop and reflect** through the use of self-coaching questions that will enable you to learn from your own experiences.

IT'S TIME FOR A SEA CHANGE

Our understanding of and beliefs about leadership have evolved over time and there seems to be another change in the wind—a growing recognition of the important qualities that introverted leaders bring to organizations. In the past leaders were expected to be heroic and charismatic authority figures. Today, as we will see in Chapter 2, successful leaders have very different qualities and are more likely to be humble and collaborative in their approach. This is not a small, incremental change, but something with huge implications for choosing and hiring people for leadership positions.

There has never been a better time to be a leader who can be vulnerable, humble, and reflective. In other words, there has never been a better time to be a leader if you are an introvert.

CHAPTER SUMMARY

- Despite representing 50% of the general population there is still a lot of confusion about introverts and introversion.

- The introverted brand is unique and worth promoting.

- Recent research shows that introverts make effective leaders in times of rapid change.

- Dynamic introverts are poised to fill the leadership gap left by retiring baby boomers.

- It takes courage to lead and dynamic introverts will do this by becoming conscious of who they are and by developing their quiet leadership skills.

- It is time to rethink the way we look at introverts and to recognize and celebrate the introverts amongst us.

CHAPTER TWO
The Power of Introverted Leaders

> "RESEARCHERS ARE FINDING THAT INTROVERTS MAKE BETTER LEADERS THAN EXTROVERTS FOR ONE SIMPLE REASON: THEY'RE MORE LIKELY TO LISTEN AND PAY ATTENTION TO WHAT OTHER PEOPLE ARE SAYING."[1]
> Susan Krauss Whitbourne

One of my objectives in writing this book is to encourage readers to challenge their outdated beliefs about introverts and leadership.

Over the past thirty years, studies looking at the percentage of introverts versus extroverts in leadership positions indicate that extroverts far outnumber introverts. These findings only add to the belief that extroverts are superior leaders.

In 2009, Adam Grant, a professor of management at Wharton College, with colleagues Francesca Gino and David Hofmann, discovered an interesting link between personality type and leadership effectiveness that challenged earlier findings.[2] Grant and his colleagues demonstrated that both extroverts and introverts can be effective leaders depending on the situation and the personality types of the people that they are leading. In other words, there is a connection between personality traits and leader effectiveness but not in the sense that we have come to believe and accept.

If we were to look more closely at who is providing leadership in our organizations we might be surprised to find that many of our leaders are in fact introverts. I believe that these leaders keep their introverted personality traits hidden because in order to succeed many of them have learned to act like extroverts.

Try this experiment for yourself: start asking friends and colleagues if they are extroverts or introverts. I think you will be surprised by what you discover. Many people we assume are extroverts are really introverts who have learned how to be more sociable, assertive, and outgoing.

As you will see from the survey responses highlighted in this chapter, dynamic introverts provide a unique style of quiet leadership, one that organizations can no longer afford to overlook. We tend to be highly observant, excel at listening to what others have to say, develop close relationships with people, are good at teaming, and able to make sense of complex information if given the time to process what we are taking in.

"The leaders and managers I have worked with over long periods of time have come to trust me and see my strengths…my quiet confidence." *Survey Participant*

•

"My leadership is done quietly, passionately, and enthusiastically." *Survey Participant*

•

"I have difficulty "thinking on my feet", or responding quickly. I prefer to take time to think issues through prior to responding. Early in my career, this made it difficult to handle volatile situations. However, I have learned to use this trait to defuse situations and give everyone time to calm down...I have built wonderful teams, because my staff trust me to be fair, and to find solutions that work for as many people as possible."
Survey Participant

The responses of the fifty self-described introverts who completed my online survey suggest that there are six components that will give us the advantage that we need if we are to thrive as leaders.

I'm calling these elements ***The Six R's***:

ROLE MODELS	RESOURCES
RECOGNITION	RESPECT
RESILIENCE	RESPITE

REFLECTING ON THE SIX R'S

ROLE MODELS

Until fairly recently it was not seen as an advantage to identify oneself as an introvert. In fact, I'm constantly surprised by the number of people I talk to who tell me that they were in a "state of denial" about their introversion or that over the years they had "convinced themselves that they were extroverted". Fortunately, this is changing as more of us speak up and declare to the world that we are indeed introverts.

I was watching the Jeff Probst show while working out at the gym the other day and was interested to hear Lisa Whelchel, who starred in the popular series *The Facts of Life*[3], describe herself to the TV audience as an introvert. As a successful actor, Lisa provides a good example for other introverts interested in pursuing an acting career.

Good role models are a key component in helping us succeed no matter which career we choose but they may be even more crucial for those of us aspiring to lead.

STOP & REFLECT

- WHO ARE MY ROLE MODELS?
- HOW HAVE THEY INSPIRED ME?
- WHAT HAVE I LEARNED FROM MY ROLE MODELS?
- HOW CAN I BE A MENTOR FOR OTHER INTROVERTS?

"I think that self-evaluation was important in my leadership role because it was apparent that my focus was the health of the organization. I think that was a good model to set." *Survey Participant*

Looking back at my career I can think of a number of people who I enjoyed mentoring. You too can be a role model for other introverts and we will explore ways of doing this in later chapters.

RECOGNITION

Due to our quiet nature, our efforts often go unrecognized. But introverts need recognition as much as extroverts. More to the point, we need to be recognized and rewarded when we find the courage to step up and lead. This acknowledgement will encourage us to develop our leadership skills even further.

STOP & REFLECT

- HOW WOULD I LIKE TO BE ACKNOWLEDGED FOR THE VALUE THAT I BRING AS A LEADER?
- WHAT WOULD I LIKE MY ORGANIZATION TO DO TO RECOGNIZE INTROVERTS AS A GROUP?
- WHAT CAN I DO TO RECOGNIZE THE CONTRIBUTIONS OF OTHER INTROVERTS IN MY LIFE?
- WHAT CAN I DO TO ENSURE THAT I AM RECOGNIZED FOR THE CONTRIBUTIONS THAT I MAKE?

"Introverts are definitely not as high profile in the workplace as extroverts who tend to be noticed and rewarded more than introverts." *Survey Participant*

Being in the spot light may make you uneasy, but as I argue in Chapter Four, if you don't highlight your own performance then you may be overlooked for promotion or other opportunities that will enrich your career.

RESOURCES

Each one of us will require different resources in order to succeed in our chosen careers. When I think of resources, the words "tools of the trade" come to mind. For instance, like so many others in our society I couldn't work effectively without access to a computer. I need it as a tool to research, write and edit, as well as to communicate with family, friends, colleagues, clients and students locally and around the world.

Another important resource for introverts is quiet space so that we can spend time alone creating our best work. Being aware of our environments—noticing which environments we thrive in and which ones have a negative impact on our ability to do our best work is crucial to our success. We also need to be ready to advocate for the type of environment in which we flourish.

STOP & REFLECT

- WHAT RESOURCES DO I NEED IN ORDER TO DEVELOP AS A LEADER AND DO MY BEST WORK?
- HOW DO I FIND SPACE IN ORDER TO DO MY BEST WORK?
- WHAT WOULD THIS SPACE LOOK LIKE?
- HOW DO I CREATE MY IDEAL ENVIRONMENT?
- HOW DO I ADVOCATE FOR THE TYPE OF ENVIRONMENT THAT I NEED?

"Find people and tools to help you gain objectivity, i.e. being able to take a step back and disentangle yourself from the emotional experience." *Survey Participant*

Throughout this book you will be provided with information about additional resources to help you develop your leadership skills. In Chapter Six you are encouraged to create a personal leadership development plan or PLDP. As part of the PLDP you will be asked to highlight your strengths to help you paint a clearer picture of who you are as a leader. When you act on your strengths in a way that is authentic you'll discover that people respect you and want to follow you.

RESPECT

We all need to be treated with respect but if we want other people to respect us we must first respect ourselves. By recognizing that we are introverts and accepting our quiet strengths we will find it easier to stand up for what we believe in. Our beliefs are the assumptions that we make about the world around us. For example, I believe that most people are good and kind and this assumption guides me when I meet someone new.

STOP & REFLECT

- HOW DO MY QUIET STRENGTHS SHOW UP?
- WHAT DO I BELIEVE IN?
- HOW HAVE I BEEN ABLE TO REMAIN TRUE TO MYSELF WHEN PRESSURED TO BE MORE LIKE OTHERS?
- WHAT ARE MY VALUES AND HOW DO I USE THESE AS A GUIDE WHEN MAKING DIFFICULT DECISIONS?

"Sometimes my introspection is seen as inactivity or passivity. Other people are always telling me how I should be." *Survey Participant*

Beliefs and values have subtle differences. Our values are the things that we deem important and that influence the decisions we make in our lives. Understanding one's values is an important leadership skill and I have provided some additional questions to help you explore your values in this chapter and again in Chapter Six.

A belief, on the other hand, is something that we think is true and that we may accept without question.

Our beliefs are influenced by many things including,

- our own personal experiences
- what our parents and other family members taught us
- what we watch on television
- what we learn in school

Unfortunately, our beliefs about the world around us, and about ourselves, can be limiting. And once we acquire certain beliefs we rarely question them despite the fact that they may be hampering our success in life.

For example, if you believe that introverts do not make good leaders you will remind yourself of this every time you consider applying for a leadership position. You may also overlook the successful introverts that you know, believing that they must, in fact, be extroverts.

In addition to limiting your chances of success in life, continuing to hold on to limiting beliefs can also affect how resilient you are.

RESILIENCE

Resilience has been described as the ability to remain optimistic despite setbacks in our lives. We are all resilient to some degree but our capacity for bouncing back varies depending on our personal values, our beliefs, our self-confidence, our competence and our energy. As introverts, it may be even more important for us to learn how to manage our energy in order to maintain our resilience.

STOP & REFLECT

- WHAT ACTIONS CAN I TAKE TO STRENGTHEN MY OWN RESILIENCE?
- WHAT ARE MY BELIEFS ABOUT MY ABILITY TO BOUNCE BACK FROM DIFFICULT SITUATIONS?
- WHAT GIVES ME THE COURAGE TO CONTINUE IN THE FACE OF UNCERTAINTY?
- WHAT ACTIONS CAN I TAKE AS A LEADER TO STRENGTHEN THE RESILIENCY OF THE PEOPLE I LEAD?

Resilient people use their inner resources to deal with the normal challenges that life throws their way without becoming overwhelmed. You can strengthen your resilience by doing the following:

- Develop close relationships with people who are positive and who support you.

- Take care of yourself by eating a healthy diet, sleeping enough, exercising and finding things to do that are fun and relaxing.

- Learn about yourself and learn from your experiences.

- Remain optimistic by focusing on your future and creating a plan to get you where you want to go.

- Focus on your accomplishments and achievements no matter how small or how large.

RESPITE

Respite may seem like an odd thing to include here, but in order to succeed in our leadership roles introverts must first acknowledge the need for short periods of rest and relief. Whether we need a physical break, time to meditate or just quiet space to reflect and process what we are learning, dynamic introverts need time for respite throughout the day.

STOP & REFLECT

- HOW CAN I BUILD RESPITE INTO MY DAILY LIFE?
- HOW CAN I LISTEN TO WHAT MY BODY NEEDS?
- WHAT CAN I DO TO LET THOSE CLOSE TO ME KNOW ABOUT MY NEED FOR RESPITE?
- HOW CAN I ENSURE THAT MY NEED FOR RESPITE IS MET?

"The public jobs rob my energy and I need lots of time to recoup." *Survey Participant*

These conversations with colleagues or superiors may be difficult at first; however, the more that people become aware of our unique needs for quiet time the more accepting they will become.

THE CHALLENGES OF LEADERSHIP

There is an age-old debate about whether leaders are made or leaders are born. I believe strongly that we are all born with the potential to be leaders. Skills can be learned and the leaders who stand out will have taken the time to develop their unique talents and will continue to develop these strengths throughout their lives.

This is the premise behind *The Leadership Challenge*[4] written by James M. Kouzes and Barry Z. Posner. What I like about this book is that it is based on 30 years of research and focuses on the experiences of a wide range of leaders: men and women, young and old, and volunteers and paid employees.

Although Kouzes and Posner did not study introverts and extroverts per se, their research supports the growing argument that organizations need all types of leaders.

Through their research, Kouzes and Posner have identified five main areas which great leaders make a point of developing. These practices include modelling the way, inspiring a shared vision, challenging the process, enabling others to act, and encouraging the heart. As leaders, we will get better and better the more we incorporate these practices into our daily lives.

BEING SELF-AWARE

In any leadership role, people will be watching to see if you do what you say you are going to do. Being self-aware and being able to self-manage is crucial to becoming an authentic and respected leader.

A number of books and courses on leadership encourage us to clarify our values. Knowing what is important—what we stand for—will make it easier for us to find the courage to speak up when it matters. The following questions are meant to help you reflect on what is important to you:

STOP & REFLECT

- WHAT AM I PASSIONATE ABOUT?
- WHAT DO I CARE ABOUT?
- WHAT DO I STAND FOR?
- HOW CAN I USE MY VALUES TO SET AN EXAMPLE AT WORK, AT HOME, AND IN MY COMMUNITY?

Being passionate about something that is important to us makes it possible to step out of our comfort zones and take a stand on what we believe in.

WHAT IS YOUR VISION?

One of the key factors in creating shared visions is to listen to other people so that they feel that they have been heard and then to incorporate what they have told you into the future direction of your team or organization.

Some years ago I attended a presentation by the CEO of a large restaurant chain in British Columbia. This executive described the process that he had used to create a collective vision for his organization. Over a three-year period he visited each of the restaurants in the chain to hear directly from employees about their vision for the future of the organization. When an audience member asked him if he would do anything differently if he repeated this exercise, the CEO replied that he would have taken even more time to sit down and listen to what the employees had to say. His approach seems to be working—the organization has one of the highest employee retention rates in the restaurant industry.

Before you engage others in creating a shared vision you might want to answer the following questions about your own vision of the future:

STOP & REFLECT

- WHAT EXCITES ME MOST ABOUT THE FUTURE?
- HOW WOULD I DESCRIBE MY IDEAL WORK COMMUNITY?
- HOW CAN I DESIGN MY IDEAL FUTURE?
- HOW CAN I INVOLVE OTHERS IN SHARING THEIR DREAMS FOR THE FUTURE?

Listening comes naturally to the introvert. As dynamic introverts, our challenge will be to engage other people in conversations about what matters to them, how they see the future, and how they want to contribute to a shared vision going forward.

QUESTIONING THE PROCESS

Perhaps one of the most crucial—and most difficult—aspects of being a leader is the need to continually question the status quo. Most of us don't like constant change but we risk losing out on opportunities to grow if we refuse to consider alternatives. This need to be open to change applies to individuals as well as teams, organizations and communities.

Change can evoke feelings of fear or powerlessness. But it is also a fact of life and leaders are in the business of helping people and organizations change successfully.

STOP & REFLECT

- WHY IS CHALLENGING THE PROCESS DIFFICULT?
- WHEN HAVE I CHALLENGED THE PROCESS? WAS I SUCCESSFUL? WHAT DID I LEARN ABOUT MYSELF?
- IN WHAT SITUATIONS WOULD I FIND IT EASY TO CHALLENGE THE PROCESS?
- IN WHAT SITUATIONS WOULD I FIND IT DIFFICULT TO CHALLENGE THE PROCESS?
- WHAT ADVICE WOULD I GIVE TO OTHER INTROVERTS TO MAKE IT EASIER FOR THEM TO CHALLENGE THE STATUS QUO?

Leaders challenge people to do things differently: to search for opportunities, to experiment and to be courageous.

ENGAGING OTHERS

Effective leadership is about enabling others to contribute the best of their experience, skills and knowledge. This is really only possible if people can see where they fit in and how they can participate. In order to be fully engaged, people need opportunities for personal development: coaching, mentoring and training are examples.

In his book, *Quiet Leadership*[5], David Rock provides a strong argument for a "new management model" based on coaching conversations. I was first drawn to this book because of the title, and although not written specifically for introverts, Rock's new management model is a good fit.

Whether you are new to leadership or a seasoned executive, coaching is a tool you can use to help people improve their thinking and thereby their performance. The coaching process requires that we slow down, stop talking and reflect. As introverts we also bring the capacity to listen deeply to the people we are coaching. After one coaching session my client emailed me back to say that she felt "heard".

STOP & REFLECT

- HOW COMFORTABLE AM I WITH SHARING LEADERSHIP WITH MY COLLEAGUES?
- WHAT CAN I DO TO DEVELOP MY QUIET LEADERSHIP STYLE?
- HOW CAN I SHARE MY GIFTS AND TALENTS WITH OTHERS?
- WHO ELSE BENEFITS WHEN I STEP UP AND LEAD?

Enabling others to act involves sharing leadership with those you work with in pursuit of a common vision and goals.

PROVIDING ENCOURAGEMENT

Encouraging the heart is about recognizing and rewarding the people we work with: our employees, volunteers and peers. This is one area in which introverts can excel as we are sensitive to the energy of others, listen well and are attuned to important details of people's lives.

Introverts and extroverts may differ in the ways that they want to be recognized. Extroverts are often happy to be recognized publicly—perhaps even expecting this kind of celebration—whereas introverts may want to be recognized individually and in private. The most effective recognition must be authentic and given in the moment, not after the moment has passed.

In the course of my career I was part of a human resources team responsible for creating an employee recognition program. At that time we asked employees how they wanted to be recognized for doing great work. Most of them replied that they wanted feedback directly from their immediate supervisor. Take some time to think about what recognition means to you:

STOP & REFLECT

- WHAT STANDS OUT AS THE MOST MEANINGFUL RECOGNITION THAT I HAVE EVER RECEIVED?
- WHAT MADE THIS MEANINGFUL TO ME AT THAT TIME?
- HOW HAVE I RECOGNIZED A COLLEAGUE IN THE PAST?
- WHAT CAN I DO TO ENSURE THAT PEOPLE ARE RECOGNIZED IN A WAY THAT IS MEANINGFUL TO THEM?

The ideas described in this chapter include important skills that we can learn. But leadership is more than a collection of skills; it is the sum total of many elements, including:

- Our values (what is important to us)

- Our history (people and events that made us who we are today)

- Our strengths (the things we are good at)

- Our personality (our introverted or extroverted traits)

- Our challenges (the things we need to improve on)

- Our mission or purpose in life (the things we are passionate about)

- Our legacy (what we want to be remembered for)

Our goal will be to weave these elements together and create our own unique leadership style.

LEADERSHIP CHALLENGES FOR INTROVERTS

As I worked on this book, I repeatedly heard stories about the challenges faced by introverts who are in leadership positions or who aspire to become leaders in their organizations and communities. If you are an introvert and find leadership challenging you are certainly not alone. In fact, it seems that a majority of us (introverts and extroverts) do not feel confident in our ability to lead. According to blogger Dan McCarthy, "1 out of 3 leaders regretted being promoted due to not knowing how to proceed."[6]

Early on in my career I could not imagine myself as a manager and I had no intention of applying for a promotion. In fact, when I was asked by a senior leader to take on a temporary management position I initially declined. I was working as a medical social worker at the time and did not believe that I had the competencies that the position required. I lacked the confidence to step into the leadership role that was being offered to me.

What happened to me in that situation happens to all of us at some time or another but it can be especially challenging for introverts when we are asked to do something we have never done before.

When we consider stepping into a leadership role it is natural to compare our image of how we see ourselves now with an image of our future self. If there is a match between the two images we will feel more confident moving ahead. However, if we are unable to imagine our future selves as leaders, we will lack the necessary confidence that enables us to take action.

When your self-confidence is low and you are feeling discouraged consider the following words from author and leadership expert Neal Burgis, "introverts are among the most successful people in the world and about 70 percent of CEO's describe themselves as introverts."[7]

We can also get into the trap of blaming organizations for not making it a priority to identify, train, and promote introverts. However, as one of my survey participants pointed out, introverts may be just as guilty for not promoting themselves:

> "Introverts are definitely not as high profile in the workplace as extroverts who tend to be noticed and rewarded more than introverts…Introverts often seem to be "ignored" or passed over because they are not as visible as extroverts. Perhaps that is partly an introvert's fault by expecting others to be just as observant as we are not pointing out our strengths and aptitudes to management when we could. Not promoting myself to management has been a definite detriment to advancement in some situations. Self-promotion is something I had to learn and become comfortable with over time." *Survey Participant*

Stop for a moment and reflect on what leadership means to you.

STOP & REFLECT

- HOW WOULD I DESCRIBE MYSELF AS A LEADER?
- HOW COMFORTABLE AM I BEING CALLED A LEADER?
- HOW CONFIDENT AM I WITH MY LEADERSHIP SKILLS?
- WHAT LEADERSHIP SKILLS DO I NEED TO DEVELOP?
- HOW CAN I PROMOTE MYSELF?

Self-promotion, although necessary for all leaders, is perhaps more difficult for introverts. Chapter Four offers an in-depth exploration of this aspect of leadership.

Not surprisingly, a number of challenges faced by introverts are related to communication with others. Here are some comments from survey participants:

- Being drowned out by more assertive/aggressive coworkers

- Not finding the right words and ideas until too late

- Not being asked our opinion

- Finding it problematic to get "air time" in meetings

- Lacking the confidence to offer ideas and opinions when the opportunity arises

- Missing in-the-moment opportunities to speak up/act

- Difficulty making ourselves heard and understood

As if these challenges aren't bad enough on their own, they also contribute to the negative perception of introverts as poor communicators. The examples in this chapter from the survey participants demonstrate the frustration faced by introverts who are not listened to and find themselves seemingly without a voice.

Conversely, we may frustrate colleagues because we don't communicate clearly or on a regular basis. I know I've been guilty of keeping my ideas and my thoughts to myself when I could have been sharing them with colleagues.

"I would say that my biggest strategy in response to my introversion is simply communication. One on one discussions and constant communication let everyone know where they stand and what plans are in the future." *Survey Participant*

FINDING OUR VOICE

"CREATORS OF ANY KIND MUST FIND THEIR VOICE.
WE ARE WRITERS, MUSICIANS, DESIGNERS, PROGRAMMERS,
PARENTS, BUILDERS OF ANYTHING.
BUT WE ARE NOT TRULY EXPRESSING OURSELVES,
AND SPEAKING THE TRUTH, UNTIL WE'VE FOUND OUR VOICE:
THE TONE, STYLE, TENOR, PITCH, PERSONALITY
WE USE TO EXPRESS OURSELVES."
Leo Babauta[8]

Leaders are also creators. We create relationships, organizations, visions, teams, campaigns, projects and new ventures. Finding our voice is one of the most profound tests that we introverts face.

> "I find busy meeting situations to be very difficult. I often have things to say, but can't speak fast enough to have my opinions heard. What I do now is raise my hand when I have something to say. Often, even that is not noticed and the conversation continues to move forward. When there is a break in the conversation, or when the chair acknowledges my hand, I simply take the conversation back to the point it was at when I had something to contribute. Over time, I find that groups tend to become more attentive and respond faster when I raise my hand." *Survey Participant*

I too have found myself raising my hand in meetings in order to be heard over the roar of competing voices and ideas. Public speaking, giving formal presentations and being asked to speak on the spur-of-the moment has been difficult for me throughout my career. With the support of Toastmasters, and repeated practice, I have become a more confident communicator.

Many dynamic introverts make it a priority to learn public speaking.

And, although there are different ways of learning these skills, I believe that active membership in an organization such as Toastmasters International[9] is a necessity for introverted leaders. Many people think that the mission of Toastmasters is to assist people to become better at public speaking but this is only part of the equation. The organization also provides a wide variety of ongoing opportunities to develop its members' leadership skills.

Early in my career, when I had decided to take steps to become more extroverted, I had no idea how hard it would be or how long it would take me. Even before I completed my first MBTI I knew that I was quiet. I found it awkward to network with people I didn't know and challenging to speak in front of a group of colleagues at work. However, as an adult, I wasn't shy and had no difficulty travelling solo or heading off to university when the opportunity presented itself.

One of my earliest memories from college is of being terrified to speak up in class. I struggled with my fear of public speaking throughout high school and university but it was only after I became a professional social worker did I realize that I had to take action. I couldn't continue attending meetings in which I was too terrified to speak. Nor could I endure the sleepless nights I spent before I had to lead a meeting or give a talk.

The ability to speak publically with confidence is a skill that is more often associated with extroversion than introversion despite the fact that extroverts fear public speaking as much as introverts.

In addition to becoming a more confident speaker, participating in Toastmasters on a regular basis can also help us learn to deal with conflict, communicate assertively, facilitate groups/teams and feel more in control during job interviews.

I think that one of the most challenging experiences that we face as introverts is the job interview. We may find ourselves at a disadvantage when we it comes to answering questions because we tend to pause and think about our answers, making us seem less than enthusiastic.

Does this mean that we are destined to miss out on finding the perfect job or advancing in our careers? Not at all, but we will have to learn how to respond to questions more quickly. One of the most effective ways of learning how to do this is by participating in what Toastmasters calls Table Topics. Table Topics is a regular feature of every meeting and a part of the agenda that people dread the most! During this portion of the meeting you will be given the opportunity to quickly organize and express your thoughts by answering a question provided by the Table Topics Master.

By participating in Table Topics regularly introverts will greatly improve their confidence and communication skills and they won't be at a loss for words during those challenging job interviews.

STEREOTYPES AND MYTHS ABOUT LEADERSHIP

The notion of the strong, authoritarian leader who speaks quickly, knows what to do, has the right answers, takes command, and solves all of our problems is a compelling one. When things are a mess we long for someone to tell us what to do. This type of leadership may be needed in a crisis but for most of us, being told what to do wears thin and we soon begin to criticize the person we hoped would make things right. This command-and-control leadership style can have devastating effects in our organizations. Bad decisions are often made and people resent being told what to do.

As well, this type of leader creates dependency. Rather than learning to solve problems and find solutions for themselves, workers in organizations led by authoritarian leaders fear making mistakes. When this happens people are less likely to take risks, try out new ideas, or speak up when something needs fixing.

LEVEL FIVE LEADERSHIP

The flip side of the loud, authoritarian leader, is a leader who is quiet and perhaps even humble. Thanks to the research of author Jim Collins, we now know that leaders who show the most empathy tend to get the best results for their organizations. The fact that quiet leaders can succeed in creating and sustaining successful organizations is perhaps one of the biggest revelations from the book *Good to Great*. Collins coined the term "Level Five Leadership" to describe these leaders.

Good to Great is based on an exploration of almost 30 successful companies that consistently outperformed their competitors over a period of two decades or longer.

There are many organizations that are good but few that ever become great—and even fewer that maintain that greatness over the long haul. Collins and his research team discovered a number of principles that must be in place in order for organizations to excel at what they do.

> *"We were surprised, shocked really, to discover the type of leadership required for turning a good company into a great one. Compared to high-profile leaders with big personalities who make head-lines and become celebrities, the good-to-great leaders seem to have come from Mars. Self-effacing, quiet, reserved, even shy—these leaders are a paradoxical blend of personal humility and professional will."*[10]

Might Collins have been describing a group of introverted leaders?

UNDERSTANDING POWER AND INFLUENCE

There is a lot written about power and influence in leadership books and in books about organizational behaviour but until recently there was very little written about "quiet power."

"Why *shouldn't* quiet be strong?"[11] asks Susan Cain in the introduction to her best-selling book *Quiet: The Power of Introverts in a World That Can't Stop Talking.*

Cain opens her book with the story of Rosa Parks, who in 1955 refused to give up her seat on a bus in Montgomery, Alabama. Her quiet act of defiance triggered a year-long boycott of Montgomery buses by the African-American citizens of that city. In the end Parks' actions led to the integration of buses when the boycott ended.

Power doesn't have to be loud and aggressive. In fact, David Hawkins, author of the book *Power VS Force* defines power as being associated with compassion.[12]

If introverted leaders tend to be more humble and quiet, compared with extroverted leaders, how do we understand and use our power? Here are some questions to get you started thinking about your use of power:

STOP & REFLECT

- WHAT DOES PERSONAL POWER MEAN TO ME?
- HOW MIGHT I USE MY PERSONAL POWER TO BEST SERVE OTHERS?
- HOW COMFORTABLE AM I WITH THE USE OF POWER?
- WHERE DO I GIVE MY POWER AWAY AND TO WHOM?

Understanding power is essential to becoming an effective leader because power and influence are two sides of the same coin. Power is something we use every single day. In fact power is the *energy* we need to move our cars, move ourselves, and keep our homes and organizations running smoothly. Leaders who use their power to benefit others tend to engage people in their organizations to develop collaborative visions, values and goals.

As leaders, our power will come from doing work that we believe in and by having a strong purpose and clear sense of our personal values. This kind of power will give us the confidence we need so that others will want to work with us. It will also make it much easier for us to deal with conflict.

CONFLICT

Conflict is a normal part of life and it is certainly a factor in the life of any organization. As a leader you will be expected to understand and deal with conflict on a regular basis. Ralph H. Kilmann, co-author with Kenneth W. Thomas of the *Thomas Kilman Conflict Mode Instrument* (TKI), suggested to me in an email exchange that we have "habitual ways of approaching conflict situations."[13]

Kilmann and Thomas have identified five modes of conflict to help us become aware of how we experience conflict:

- Competing
- Collaborating
- Compromising
- Avoiding and
- Accommodating

By taking the TKI survey[14] we can become aware of which mode or modes we use too often or not at all. As dynamic introverts, our goal is to understand how we typically resolve differences and how all five modes can be useful in resolving conflict, depending on the situations we find ourselves in.

Conflict, if handled with sensitivity, can be a catalyst for positive change and growth. If not handled properly, it can have the opposite effect: leaving people feeling angry, misunderstood and powerless.

When students in my leadership classes discover their habitual approach to dealing with conflict through the TKI survey, they are often disappointed because they believe that their approach is not the most effective one. There is nothing inherently wrong with any of the conflict modes and in fact all of them are necessary or useful at any given point. The challenge is to be able to move from one position to another depending on the situation.

This knowledge underlines the importance of learning conflict resolution skills. One of the best on-line resources that I've utilized is the Conflict Resolution Network, an Australian website[15] where you can access free training materials and up-to-date information and resources.

Being an introvert may also mean that you have certain traits or skills that will make you exceptionally good at resolving conflict. Two excellent tools at your disposal as a dynamic introvert are your ability to listen so that people feel they have been heard and your ability to recognize that people need space and time to come up with their own answers.

When I was the leader of a geriatric health care program in the 1990s, I supervised three employees who sometimes had disagreements about their work. About every six months or so one of them would come to my office asking me for assistance because their lack of consensus was negatively affecting their performance. I would invite the three of them to a meeting and then sit back and listen. We didn't have any formal ground rules but I made certain that each of them were able to voice their concerns.

They always came to an agreement that worked for all of them. My role was to create a safe space for them to talk respectfully and to listen to each other.

Listening attentively is one of the skills that introverts bring to the role of leader and it is a quality that often differentiates us from extroverts.

LEADERSHIP, REFLECTION & LEARNING

Perhaps the most important leadership skill is the ability to stop and reflect before taking action. Reflection leads to better problem solving, better decisions, and enhanced learning. But as introverts are discovering, "Society gives reflection and its counterpart—listening—short shrift."[16] In our hyperactive world, stopping to reflect on one's experience can be taken as a sign of weakness. Take note that it can also be confused with procrastination.

WHAT CHALLENGES DO INTROVERTS FACE IN THE WORKPLACE?

"Quick decision making models—no information, no time to think. Challenging to get airtime when the majority are extroverted. I find it hard to speak over people and interrupt." *Survey Participant*

•

"I feel railroaded sometimes by the extroverts. It is like they have a train going and I don't want to be on it, but they think I can be on it. I need time and space and the extroverts are so loud and fast." *Survey Participant*

When I was a university student I would often find a sudden interest in cleaning my apartment. Was I reflecting on my schoolwork? Probably not—what I was doing was avoiding it by procrastinating.

I know I am not alone. Many people procrastinate by keeping busy doing things to fill the time. I think the emphasis here is on keeping busy so we don't have time to stop and reflect. Stopping to reflect ensures that we can focus more clearly on what we are doing.

An environment which encourages reflection would be an asset in most organizations. Imagine physical space such as private offices for quiet time as well as opportunities to break during meetings to catch up with our thoughts. The ability to reflect comes naturally to introverts and it is this ability that organizations need to recognize and encourage.

LEARNING ORGANIZATIONS

The type of environment that encourages reflection is often referred to as a *learning organization*, a concept that was first introduced by Peter Senge in the 1990s in *The Fifth Discipline*.[17] A primary focus for a learning organization is on learning together. The emphasis is on learning collaboratively as a team or as an entire organization or community group. Learning organizations require leaders who make this a priority, listen well and use a coaching approach at least some of the time. Learning organizations also provide supportive environments that encourage time for reflection both for individuals and for groups.

A great many books and articles have been written about the learning organization since *The Fifth Discipline* was first published. Many books focus on the tools that learning organizations use to make shared learning a reality."[18] One of these tools, dialogue, is a powerful form of communication that relies on listening, self-awareness and self-management.

This type of group communication encourages participants to slow down, be in the moment and really listen to what everyone is saying. It is often used in situations where there is a conflict.

When I first read about dialogue the idea really resonated with me. This might have been because, as an introvert, I struggled to have my voice heard in most of the meetings I attended.

Dialogue is an often overlooked facilitation tool that enhances learning and makes it possible for everyone involved to share their ideas and experiences. Dialogue is easy to learn but it takes a bit of practice to be able to use it effectively!

Here is a list of ground rules that I have used when asked to facilitate a dialogue session:

- Listen and speak without judgement
- Acknowledge each speaker
- Respect differences
- Suspend your role and status
- Avoid cross talk
- Focus on learning
- Check your assumptions

If you are an introvert and want to change the way your meetings are run, I would encourage you to introduce the idea of dialogue and offer to organize and lead the first session. And as an introvert you will most likely have the advantage when it comes to using this method because you are naturally wired to slow down and listen before your speak. As a Dynamic Introvert, push yourself to go one step further by sharing what you are observing, experiencing and learning.

HOW HAS BEING AN INTROVERT AFFECTED YOUR CAREER?

"Positively because I have done so much listening and observing, I often do things right, well, thoroughly and see efficiencies and improve processes. Bosses have taken notice." *Survey Participant*

SELF-LEADERSHIP & PERSONAL MASTERY

We cannot lead others unless we can lead ourselves. This is a simple statement but it is perhaps the type of leadership most challenging to achieve because it means that we have to be honest with ourselves about who we are. Whatever we expect others to do we must be willing to do ourselves first. To reiterate Kouzes and Posner's phrase, we must "model the way" for those we lead. By continuing to learn and to develop ourselves as leaders, we can set a valuable example for others.

Peter Senge popularized the concept "personal mastery"[19] in *The Fifth Discipline*. Personal mastery is the belief that you can shape your future and the future of the group or organization in which you lead. This is a life-long journey in which we take responsibility for our development and growth as leaders who are also introverts.

There are many tools and resources that we can use to help us along this journey. In the chapters ahead, we'll take a look at what dynamic introverts can do to face specific challenges such as low energy, lack of organizational support or negative branding.

CHAPTER SUMMARY

- Many successful introverts have learned to act like extroverts in order to advance in their careers but this need will decrease as society begins to recognize introverts for their unique attributes and skills.

- The challenges introverts face can be overcome with the help of the **6 R's:** Role Models, Resources, Recognition, Resilience, Respect, and Respite.

- Researchers such as Adam Grant, Francesca Gino, David Hofmann, Jim Kouzes, Barry Posner and Jim Collins make a strong argument for leadership diversity and the importance of quiet, humble leaders.

- Listening and reflecting are two key leadership skills that introverts excel at.

- Dynamic introverts can tap into their quiet power by connecting with their passion and by knowing and living true to their values and their life purpose.

- Introverts' quiet strengths make them effective at resolving conflict.

CHAPTER THREE
The Energy Equation

"THE BIGGEST DIFFERENT BETWEEN PEOPLE
WHO GET WHAT THEY WANT OUT OF LIFE AND
PEOPLE WHO DON'T IS ENERGY."
Mira Kirshenbaum[1]

Early one morning, I was sitting on the sofa, watching the news and drinking coffee. It was a cold, drab day in the Pacific Northwest and I was not feeling very energetic! Then, in quick succession, I answered phone calls from two of my more outgoing friends wanting to make plans for that evening. After the second call I noticed how my energy levels had improved dramatically.

Over the years I have learned to pay attention to my own energy. I am known to screen phone calls, especially when my energy levels are low. But, I've also learned that sometimes I need to connect with other people in order to recharge my batteries.

Indeed, how introverts access and manage energy is one of the main characteristics that differentiate us from extroverts. The two personality groups sit at opposite ends of the energy continuum. Introverts prefer to focus inwardly in order to re-energize while extroverts boost their energy by focusing on the world around them.

Many definitions of introversion emphasize how we draw energy by reflecting on our inner world but like me on that dreary morning, we may also need the boost of connecting with other people.

As we will see in this chapter, an understanding of energy is necessary for dynamic introverts. We are often made to feel that we should be more like extroverts, but if we bow to pressure we may not give ourselves permission to recharge in ways that work for us.

"During my university student placements in physiotherapy, supervisors expressed concern about whether or not I had chosen the right career path because I did not want to sit with the group and socialize in the noisy hospital cafeteria during staff breaks. That feedback really affected me and made me feel that I was a lesser person because I was different. I knew then that I needed to have that time alone and away from everything/everybody in order to recharge for the rest of the day." *Survey Participant*

Introverts have unique challenges when it comes to managing energy. For instance, because of the way our brains are wired, we are already highly stimulated.[2] If we don't learn to recognize when this is happening and find ways to cut down on external stimulation, we can find ourselves in the midst of an energy crisis that may have been preventable.

What's the first thing that comes to mind when you hear the word "energy crisis"? Many of you will immediately think about the limited supplies of oil and gas in the world.

It's hard not to think about energy in this way as we are constantly reminded of the amount of fossil fuel available and the growing demand worldwide.

But the dwindling amount of fossil fuel available to satisfy our lifestyles is not the only energy crisis that we should be paying attention to. I believe that we, as a society, are in the midst of a worldwide personal energy crisis.

What, exactly, do I mean by energy and how do we get more of it? Or, as organizational energy researchers Heike Bruch, Brend Vogel and Felicitas Morhar ponder, "How to grasp a force which is powerful but rather invisible?"[3] These questions intrigued me so I decided to delve deeper into the subject of personal energy and its implications for introverts.

DIFFERENT TYPES OF ENERGY

Chi is a Chinese word meaning aliveness, life force energy, or life breath. Chi is also known as Ki, Qi, or Prana in other Asian cultures. This ancient concept is only now gaining a mainstream level of understanding in the West.

In *The Emotional Energy Factor*, Mira Kirshenbaum categorizes energy as either physical or emotional. Through her research she has determined that about a third of our energy is physical in nature and the rest of it is emotional. Emotional energy is described as "an aliveness of mind, a happiness of heart, and a spirit filled with hope."[4]

We can increase our physical energy by exercising, eating nutritious foods, sleeping six to eight hours a night, drinking plenty of water, and limiting the amount of alcohol we consume.

According to Kirshenbaum, most of us are finding that emotional energy is in short supply and she notes that this is the primary reason that people visit their physicians.

Authors Jim Loehr and Tony Swartz also have some recommendations to boost personal energy in *The Power of Full Engagement*.[5] The book, along with the Full Engagement Training System, is based on what the authors have learned while working with athletes and business leaders.

Our physical energy, argue Loehr and Swartz, provides us with the foundation without which we cannot achieve full capacity in all areas of our lives: the mental, the emotional, and the spiritual. In other words, when we are stressed, out of shape, tired, and not eating properly, it is more challenging to connect with others, focus our thinking or align ourselves with our purpose.

Perhaps the most valuable message I took away from *The Power of Full Engagement* is the need to balance both stress and recovery. We need to stress our bodies by challenging ourselves mentally and physically but we also need to find time to rest.

As dynamic introverts we need to learn how to pulse—to move between spending energy and renewing energy and we need to learn how to do this *consciously* if we want to be successful leaders. By pulsing we can keep our energy up throughout the day rather than allowing ourselves to run down. Think of yourself as a rechargeable battery. Every few hours you may need to stop what you are doing and tap into an energy source.

Becoming conscious of our energy requirements and being able to manage our personal energy will powerfully impact the ways in which we deal with the challenges that we will inevitably find ourselves facing as leaders.

The following questions will help you to better understand and control your personal energy:

STOP & REFLECT

- DO I HAVE THE ENERGY TO ACHIEVE THE GOALS THAT I AM AIMING FOR?
- WHEN DO I NEED THE MOST ENERGY? FOR WHICH ACTIVITIES?
- WHEN IS MY ENERGY AT ITS HIGHEST?
- WHAT AM I DOING WHEN I FEEL MOST ENERGIZED? WHAT ENERGIZES ME?
- WHERE DO I GET MY ENERGY?
- WHAT DRAINS MY ENERGY?
- HOW CAN I RECHARGE WHEN MY BATTERY IS LOW?
- WHAT AM I TOLERATING?

This is a bit like sleuthing. You may need to put your detective hat on to discover the answers to these questions.

As a coach, "what are you tolerating in your life?" is a question that I often ask my clients. People seek out coaching because they want more energy and it is difficult to feel energized when you are weighed down by things that you are allowing to control your life. Another way of looking at this is to visualize a large, invisible sack that you are carrying around with you. The amount and type of "stuff" that may be included in your sack is unlimited but I've been told by my clients that they feel weighted down by the following:

- Unresolved issues from the past

- Old habits that no longer serve a useful purpose

- Negative emotions about people or events

- Focusing on past failures

These are some examples of the "baggage" that you might be tolerating or find that you can't let go of. Of course we all tolerate things that we know we shouldn't: jobs that are boring or that don't challenge us anymore, relationships that are toxic or behaviours (our own and others) that no longer serve us.

But there is another reason that introverts need to pay particular attention to this issue. According to author Marti Olsen Laney, "Genetic research has shown that it takes introverts longer than extroverts to reconstitute themselves when they are depleted."[6] Knowing this important information and acting on it may mean the difference between succeeding or failing in a job that requires a continuous outpouring of your energy.

Determining what is affecting us is the first step in understanding our energy requirements and how we might go about raising our energy levels. Because there are so many variables affecting our personal energy this may take some time but will be well worth it in the end.

TRY THIS EXERCISE

On a scale of 1—10 with 10 being fully charged and 1 being alarmingly low, rate your energy level now. If your energy is low what can you do to raise it a couple of notches? Try doing this exercise through-out the day to get a handle on your energy at different times and in different situations.

I recommend that you use a journal, note book, smart phone or other electronic device to keep track of what you are learning about yourself. This information will provide you with a baseline showing you when your energy is low and when it is at its peak. Once you are armed with this information you can experiment with ways of consciously recharging when your body needs to recover.

My own energy levels are typically low in the early afternoon. I have found that this is a good time for me to work with one other person or with a small group. Working alone in my office will only continue to drain me.

Whatever you discover about your energy requirements, I would encourage you to try something new, something that you haven't done before, and to keep track of the effect it has on you.

"I always enjoyed working late when the rest of the staff left so I could focus and breathe. Now I realize I should have just closed the door. I spent a lot of time thinking about work at home. I woke up early trying to problem solve the day's agenda." *Survey Participant*

•

"I know I need my reflection time. After teaching all day I need to reflect in the evening." *Survey Participant*

ALONE TIME

In the on-line survey I conducted in 2012 I asked participants how and where they had found respite when they were running low on energy. Alone time, or solitude as it is often called, is a basic human need. As Tina Coleman writes, "introverts feel a greater need for solitude than extroverts do."[7] If we are to succeed as leaders in our fast-paced society we must learn to recognize and honour this need.

"I take "days off". I disconnect from others and go to a park or hike, read a book or stay alone at home while everybody else is working or at school." *Survey Participant*

> "A complete change of scenery, ALONE, and going to the water's edge or better yet, out on the water. Fuel and comfort for my soul." *Survey Participant*

What constitutes alone time for one person will be different for someone else. While it may not be possible for many of us to take a day off, finding time out to be alone—even as little as a five-minute break—at some point during the day is essential for introverts.

We need time to process all of the information that we are taking in through our senses. We may also need to be alone after we have pushed ourselves to do something that takes us outside our comfort zone. This time for self-reflection helps us to make sense of the world. It also enables us to collect our thoughts either before or after we engage in work that is mentally taxing.

As we saw in Chapter Two, finding respite throughout the day gives us the advantage we need to succeed as leaders.

LEADERS NEED ABUNDANT ENERGY

The demands of the 21st century are complex and we can be sure that our personal energy resources will be put to the test. As leaders, we are on all the time. As I sat down to write this book, this was the image that came to mind. You may be a teacher, a parent, or leader in an organization; whatever your role, people will look to you for direction and for information about possible changes that will affect them and their security. In fact, studies show that even when leaders are not talking they are watched more carefully than anyone else.[8]

The fact that leaders are expected to be on all the time should be argument enough for our need for periods of solitude. In fact the opposite has happened and over the past thirty years opportunities to stop and reflect at work have all but disappeared.

In the 1980s I worked for the City of Vancouver as part of an interdisciplinary team providing long term care services to people with chronic health problems. In those days it was not unusual for me to return to the office to find a colleague quietly reading a professional journal. We also took our coffee and lunch breaks as scheduled and our employer encouraged us to take time off to continue our professional development through seminars and workshops.

A decade later things were beginning to change and not for the better. Referring to the workplace in general, Ester Buchholz remarked in 1998 that "breaks in the workday are rapidly disappearing".[9]

And ten years after that, breaks became almost non-existent, at least for those in leadership or managerial positions in the organization I worked for. Actual coffee breaks were replaced by coffee provided to leaders during meetings. Lunch was hurriedly eaten at one's desk or if we were required to attend a meeting during our lunch breaks the organization provided us with something to eat.

What can introverted leaders do to make space to renew their energy? We can start by being clear about our needs and by communicating this to others. Instead of saying that we need time on our own we can be specific in explaining why, e.g. "I need 30 minutes without interruption to review the meeting that we just had." "I need 15 minutes on my own to review a project that I'm working on" or "I've had back-to-back meetings all morning and I need to go for a walk at lunchtime." If you are not used to asking for time to think, you may want to practice a few times with someone you know and feel comfortable with.

If you can slot some respite time into your week, either during or after work, and tell people that these commitments are non-negotiable, you will find that your energy levels improve. Asking for what you need may seem impossible at first, but as we will see in Chapter Seven there is a growing awareness in society that we all need to slow down and take time out.

ORGANIZATIONAL ENERGY

Up until now we've been talking primarily about individual energy. But, in the workplace, we all need to engage with other people on a regular basis. Energy makes it possible for individuals, teams and entire organizations to accomplish the work that needs to be done. Somehow we all need to find a balance between being alone and being with others. As leaders we are stewards of organizational energy and we must manage our own energy in such a way that we can inspire and energize others.[10]

When I mentioned to a friend that I was writing this book she shared a story about two principals who had worked at her children's school. The first, an extrovert by nature, was visible, enjoyed getting to know the students and the parents, and was generally well liked. He never missed an opportunity to participate in school events in the evenings and on weekends. When he left the school he was replaced by an extremely introverted man who rarely left his office. He became known as the no fun principal.

My first reaction to this story was that the members of the school community were judging the new principal unfairly. However, upon reflection, I concluded that since he had taken on this high profile role he really needed to flex his extroverted muscles. This flexing is also referred to as "pseudo extroversion".[11]

> "Yes, I am a pseudo extrovert. I like times when I am immersed in a group of people, DEPENDING on the vibe. I love being alone and reading and doing my art and meditating." *Survey Participant*

While necessary at times, taking on roles that push us out of our comfort zones can be energy draining and requires self-awareness and strategies to help us recover. For years I ate my lunch alone in my office, not realizing that I was looking after myself by seeking respite from the constant demands of my job.

I think we can all agree that poor leadership saps organizational energy. The introverted school principal in the situation described above may have had great leadership skills but by hiding in his office his actions had a powerful effect on the energy of the school whether or not he was aware of it.

Many of us feel as if we are leading dual lives but this is especially true for introverts who present one person at home and a different person when they are out in public.

This behaviour of course refers to our need to be more extroverted in order to succeed in the world and then revert to our natural behaviour once out of the spotlight.

> "Since I truly admired in some way extroverts, I could pretend to be one…In fact, many people from my past may classify me as an extrovert. Small wonder, as I worked at it for survival." *Survey Respondent.*

Leading dual lives could be a sign that we are being less than authentic. What exactly is authenticity? It means being real or genuine in how we relate to other people. Authentic people are open and honest and are self-aware. Psychologists tell us that people who score high on authenticity also report a strong sense of self-worth, purpose, confidence and the ability to achieve their goals.

Authenticity and transparency have particular relevance for introverted leaders who need to push themselves to be more extroverted. Remember that we all have both introverted and extroverted aspects of our personalities. Those of us who are more introverted will need to push ourselves to speak up, to deal with conflict, to socialize and to advocate for what we believe in.

The key point to remember is that we need to do this in a way that is genuine. Other people are more likely to respect and listen to us if we are 'true to ourselves'. We'll come back to the topic of authenticity in Chapter Six.

"I act when I am with people. I had to learn and I still have to learn to push myself beyond my own boundaries." *Survey Participant*

•

"I don't allow myself not to do something because it makes me uncomfortable. I have one person that I check back with to make sure my interactions in groups are appropriate. I don't go straight home but have an hour where I am alone (coffee shop, in the car, book store)." *Survey Participant*

One of the potential challenges faced by introverted leaders is becoming *invisible*. We may be so good at hiding in plain sight that our ideas are ignored or we are overlooked for plum assignments or job promotions. Pushing ourselves past the boundaries we have set up for our own protection may be the best way to increase our public profile.

We all have our favorite ways of refueling. In fact there are as many different ways as there are introverts. Dr. Brian Little has coined the term "restorative niche" to describe "the place you go when you want to return to your true self".[12] On reflection, I realized that I had been observing this practice intuitively for some time. Recently I had an extremely busy week planned. I could feel my stress levels rising in anticipation. Then, as I reviewed what I had to do each day, I mentally made a note of where I would be able to stop and recharge. Once I could see where I had some free space in which I could be myself, my anxiety dropped and I felt calmer.

Sometimes it is not possible to physically leave what you are doing to find a "restorative niche." Sometimes you will have to turn inward and quiet your mind. The following quick meditation can be done sitting at your desk, or if you don't have an office with a door you can close, you may need to hide in the bathroom—something that self-described introverts such as Dr. Brian Little have been known to do.

QUICK MEDITATION—COUNTING BACKWARDS

I have found that a good way to meditate is to find a quiet place, relax, take a few deep breaths and close your eyes. In your mind simply start counting backwards from twenty-five. Do this slowly, in time with your heartbeat. Every time you get off track go back to twenty-five. When you reach one, you have completed the meditation.

CREATING YOUR IDEAL ENVIRONMENT

From the time we are born the environments in which we find ourselves have a profound impact on how we develop and who we become as adults.

When we are children we don't have much control over these environments, but we intuitively gravitate towards people and activities that are positive and nurturing and will help us grow. Like all living things we respond positively to kindness, love, good food, laughter, and supportive feedback.

As adults we have more influence over our surroundings but I believe that most of us don't give a lot of thought as to what this means for our overall satisfaction at work. As a first step I encourage you to consider the following questions:

STOP & REFLECT

- WHAT TYPE OF WORK ENVIRONMENT WOULD MAKE IT DIFFICULT FOR ME TO GET MY WORK DONE?
- WHAT DOES MY IDEAL SETTING LOOK LIKE?
- WHICH ORGANIZATIONS OR JOBS WILL PROVIDE ME WITH THIS TYPE OF ENVIRONMENT?
- WHAT TYPE OF ENVIRONMENT INSPIRES ME AND ENERGIZES ME?
- WHAT CAN I DO TO CREATE MY IDEAL SURROUNDING?
- HOW WILL I ENLIST OTHERS IN HELPING ME TO CREATE AND MAINTAIN MY IDEAL ENVIRONMENT?

An added benefit of working through the above questions is that you will be prepared to answer similar questions when they come up in your next job interview. Considering how many hours you spend at work each week finding the right "fit" makes a lot of sense. Job fit is a human resources term that includes, among other things, the personality of the person applying for the job, the duties that they are expected to perform and of course the environment in which they will be working in.

As dynamic introverts we need to create places where we can thrive. Coaches have been helping their clients create these winning environments for some time. These surroundings are not limited to physical space but can include support from family and friends as well as co-workers.

In *Quiet*, Susan Cain describes the types of environments that are conducive to both individual and group health and productivity. Citing data that shows that noisy open plan offices are not conducive to productivity, Cain observes that "…top performers overwhelmingly worked for companies that gave their employees the most privacy, personal space, control over their physical environments, and freedom from interruption."[13]

When I first read Cain's argument, I thought "hurrah!" Here is some ammunition for introverts needing to argue for their own work space.

Unfortunately not everyone agrees. In today's economic climate, companies are always looking for ways to cut expenses and open floor plans can accommodate more workers in less space. But these immediate savings may cost employers in the long run. This may be another example of short term gain at the expense of increased employee production. The questions that must be asked are, "will introverts be as productive in open offices and will they feel engaged if their needs for privacy and personal space are ignored?"

It is important to remember that, as introverts, we make up one-half of the workforce.

Dynamic introverts can provide leadership here by being advocates for alone time. As a leader, by telling people about your need to recover your energy, you in turn give other people permission to recoup theirs. This could be the beginning of a paradigm shift in your organization's culture—a shift toward improved productivity and more engaged employees.

THE IMPORTANCE OF KNOWING YOUR LIFE PURPOSE

Some people seem to be born knowing what they are meant to do; their passion provides the energy they need to accomplish their dreams. For others discovering their life purpose happens slowly over time. No matter how long it takes us to realize what we are meant to be doing with our lives, tapping into the energy that living our purpose provides can be a powerful experience. According to Richard J. Leider, purpose is "a unique source of energy."[14] This form of energy is not unlike the spiritual energy described by Jim Loehr and Tony Swartze in *The Power of Full Engagement*.

This energy does not diminish in the same way that physical energy does; in fact, it is the type of energy that introverts need if they are to take on challenges they would normally avoid, e. g. public speaking, dealing with conflict, attending networking or social events, talking with employees, or sharing their mission, vision and values.

Discovering one's life purpose has become a widely practised activity but it was not too many years ago that people didn't talk about their purpose in life. In fact, discovering one's calling or vocation was usually described as a religious or spiritual endeavour. Today, an organization will routinely develop a mission statement as an expression of what it stands for. That statement is used to guide day-to-day operations.

As individuals it is more common for us to create statements of purpose or life-purpose to describe who we are and what we stand for. I like the following definition of purpose by Richard J. Leider:

> *"Purpose is that deepest dimension within us—our central core or essence—where we have a profound sense of who we are, where we came from, and were we are going. Purpose is the quality we choose to shape our lives around. Purpose is a source of energy and direction."*[15]

As an introverted leader knowing and living your life purpose will help you to,

- Feel more energized
- Give your life meaning
- Increase flow in your life
- Develop your unique brand (more about this in Chapter 4).

It took me a long time to realize that my life purpose involves writing and sharing information and ideas with others. When I'm investigating new ideas and writing about my discoveries I feel energized and often lose track of time. I can compare this to times when I have been working on projects that have little meaning for me: they sap my energy and I've had to force myself to carry on despite the fact that I have little interest in what I'm working on.

Discovering and living your life purpose can be elusive but it is well worth the effort.

AVOIDING BURNOUT

"I have often worked in fast-paced environments where outgoing, gregarious people thrive. I love to be around extroverts and I also realize that, for me, being around such people requires energy." *Survey Participant*

As we have seen there are numerous reasons why it is important for introverts to understand and manage their energy needs. Burnout, a potential problem for introverts, can have a devastating effect on our well-being and can lead to physical and emotional problems. And according to author Adam McHugh there is some evidence that introverts are more prone to burnout than extroverts.[16]

This didn't make sense to me until recently when I met with a colleague from work. Over lunch, she commented that sometimes introverts go too far in trying to come across as extroverts. In this example her boss's behaviour swung from hiding in his office, avoiding speaking to groups of staff or clients, and avoiding conflict. In meetings, however, he seemed to lose patience quickly and often cut people off when they were speaking. It seemed to my colleague that her boss was suffering a classic case of burnout.

As Debbie talked about her situation, it became clear that this leader had little or no awareness as to how his emotional outbursts were affecting the people he worked with or the potential negative impact his behavior could have on his own health.

The term burn-out was coined in the early 1970s by psychoanalyst Herbert J. Freudenberger.[17] Burnout can be described as state of chronic stress and frustration that leads to:

- physical and emotional exhaustion

- feelings of cynicism and detachment and

- a sense of ineffectiveness and lack of accomplishment[18]

What is important to keep in mind is that once we reach this state it has negative consequences for both individuals and organizations. In the workplace burnout can lead to poor performance and high turnover.

On a personal level, burnout can lead to family or relationship problems, career derailment, and both acute and chronic health issues e.g. insomnia, headaches, weight loss or gain, substance abuse, and high blood pressure.

Although the problem of burnout applies to both introverts and extroverts, I think it is becoming more prevalent in our society and I want introverts to be aware of what they can do to prevent it from happening to them.

Burnout may be caused by the following factors. You may feel that you are not:

- Qualified for the job you are doing

- Helped to gain the knowledge and skills you need

- Given enough time to deal with all of the demands placed on you

- Supported by coworkers or your immediate supervisor

- Able to control decisions that affect your work

- Recognized for your efforts.

Not being recognized for the contributions we make can lead to a sense that not all employees are being treated fairly. Introverts may notice that extroverts are more likely to be recognized and promoted into leadership positions and this may lead to a sense of unfairness or injustice.

UNFAIRNESS

"It's easy to overlook introverts in the workplace." *Survey Participant*

In 2008 Christina Maslach, professor of psychology at the University of California, Berkeley and Michael Leiter, professor of organizational psychology at Acadia University, published the results of their research on job burnout and engagement.[19] They were interested in the question, "What determines whether or not a person will become burned out or become more engaged in their work?" They discovered that it is the perception of *fairness* that is the tipping point which determines whether people are likely to burn out.

Knowing what signs to look for and what steps you can take to prevent it is the key to avoiding burnout. Another way for introverts to avoid burnout is to develop their emotional intelligence or EQ.

EMOTIONAL INTELLIGENCE, INTROVERSION AND BURNOUT

In a 2006 research paper Stéphane Côté and Brian Golden of the University of Toronto's Rotman School of Management identified the link between introversion, EQ and burnout in managers.

Côté and Golden discovered that introverted managers who scored high on emotional intelligence were more likely to become aware that their energy was being depleted. This realization was the first step in regaining lost energy. In contrast, introverted managers with low emotional intelligence were less likely to detect that their energy was depleted and this left them unable to regain the energy that they needed. The low EQ group was more likely to suffer from emotional exhaustion.[20] This could have serious implications for introverts who may take longer than extroverts to restore their energy when it has been used up.

As we can see from Côté and Golden's research, developing our emotional intelligence is one of the most important things that we can do to prevent burnout. Self-awareness and self-management are two of the hallmarks of emotional intelligence and are crucial for detecting and preventing emotional distress in ourselves and others.

What is emotional intelligence and how do we develop it? In short, emotional intelligence is the ability to understand our own emotions and the impact that our emotions have on the people we interact with. EQ is considered a necessary set of skills for success in today's workplaces and it is especially important for leaders.

In addition, introverts should be aware that emotional distress can impact how our brains' function and that being under stress can put us at a disadvantage when it comes to communicating our thoughts and ideas.

When we are anxious or stressed our brains working memory becomes impaired. Working memory is necessary for staying focused on a task and blocking out distractions.

As a young social work student, I was asked to give an important presentation to a group of seniors living in

Vancouver. My supervisor John was on hand to introduce me and give me moral support. On the walk back to the office John assured me that the meeting had gone well but I had no way of knowing as I couldn't remember any of it. My anxiety was so strong that I had blanked out the entire meeting.

For me this was a painful example of how emotional distress can impact our mental functioning. This is what Marty Olsen Laney refers to as "brain locking"[21] when our minds go "blank" or we "can't think straight." For introverts this lapse in mental function makes it appear as if we don't know what we are talking about or that we lack the confidence to speak up.

By developing our emotional intelligence we can learn to reduce stress provoked by fear or anxiety and prevent brain locking from hindering our thinking. In addition, being in touch with and managing our emotions will make it easier for us to recover our personal energy.

TAKE ACTION TO AVOID BURNOUT

How can we prevent ourselves from becoming burned out? Or, if we are already experiencing symptoms of burnout, what can we do to lessen the effects?

Recognize The Signs of Burnout: Some introverts are more at risk for burnout than others. By becoming aware of the causes of burnout you can take action to prevent it from happening in the first place. Canadian leadership expert Lance Secretan has created a short quiz that you can use to help you begin the process.[22]

Understand Your Energy Requirements: This is especially true when you are extroverting or pushing yourself out of your comfort zone. Be sure to build in time for respite and recovery. The self-coaching questions on personal energy in this chapter will help you to focus on understanding your energy needs.

Learn to Handle Conflict: Unresolved conflict can be a source of anxiety and stress. Introverts who are conflict avoiders may find that they are surprisingly good at resolving conflict if they learn to use their listening skills. You can become aware of your approach to conflict[23] and make a conscious effort to deal with disagreements when they arise rather than trying to ignore them.

Develop and Value Your Support Network: Develop good relationships with people you work with and nurture your personal support network.

Clarify Your Values: Understand what is important to you so that you can set boundaries and say no to requests that create a conflict for you.

Develop Your Own Personal Strategies: As a dynamic introvert you can access resources to help you prevent or recover from burnout if it does occur. One example is the work of Elizabeth Bakken *Understanding and Avoiding Burnout as a Manager,* accessible through the Mindtools website.[24]

Preventing burnout is something that organizations should pay attention to because there is a lot that can be done. Here are a few suggestions:

- Ensure that everyone has the tools and resources that they need in order to do their work.

- Recognize and treat all employees fairly and with respect.

- Provide clear communication and keep employees "in the loop" especially during times of organizational change.

CHAPTER SUMMARY

- Introverts and extroverts manage their energy differently.

- Dynamic introverts must find a balance between expending their energy and renewing it.

- Introverts must be clear about their energy needs and be able to communicate this to others. In this way introverts provide much needed leadership by advocating for periods of solitude.

- Leaders are stewards of organizational energy and must pay attention to how their energy influences the energy of the people they work with.

- Burnout is a potential problem for introverts and something they can avoid or alleviate by developing their emotional intelligence.

CHAPTER FOUR
Personal Branding & Self Promotion for Introverts

"YOUR GOAL WILL BE TO LET YOUR BRAND BECOME
A VEHICLE FOR YOUR MOST AUTHENTIC SELF."
Robin Fisher Roffer[1]

It appears that personal branding is fast becoming a mainstream activity especially for those of us wanting to advance in our careers. Few introverts will greet this idea with enthusiasm since branding requires us to promote ourselves and this is the last thing that most of us want to do. Although we may not want to be the centre of attention, the reality is that if we don't brand ourselves in a way that works for us, someone else most likely will, and this may not necessarily be to our benefit.

We all project a certain image to the world and we all have a unique identity that defines who we are. If we have been working for any length of time we will also have developed a certain reputation in our community or place of work. These qualities tell the world who we are; they are the foundation of our personal brand. Having introverted or extroverted traits is a key aspect of who we are and how people perceive us. So, how can we, as dynamic introverts, use this knowledge to our advantage?

As I began doing my research for this book, I found myself curious about whether or not my friends and acquaintances were introverts or extroverts. When I raised the question several people immediately told me that they were extroverts. Interestingly, when I explained the difference, a few of them decided that they were actually introverts. I still think that some of the people I know are introverts even though they don't see themselves from that perspective.

I can't say that I blame them. "Our culture values and rewards the qualities of extroverts," writes psychologist and author Marti Olsen Laney.[2] Unfortunately, the flip side of this is that introverts may get some "bad press" as the word introvert has come to have some fairly negative meanings associated with it.

Who would want to admit to being an introvert in a society that rewards and values extroverts and sees introverts in a negative light? Here are a few of the adjectives that are commonly used to describe introverts:

- Withdrawn

- Passive

- Socially inept

- Boring

- Slow thinking

- Submissive

So you see, as a group, introverts are already branded, regardless of whether we like it or not.

As part of my research I set out to discover how I am perceived by those who know me. I emailed some close friends and colleagues and asked them the following questions:

- How would you describe my personal brand?

- If someone mentions my name what images come to mind?

These are the words that they used to describe me:

Open, well-researched, informed, focused, supportive, a writer and a reader, an information sharer, a good listener, flexible, empathetic, participatory, passionate about the cause of the organization, well read, thoughtful, open minded, calm, reasonable, dependable, approachable, good listener, negotiator, problem solver, thorough, well informed, voracious reader and researcher, compassionate, a good listener, loyal, positive reputation, puts her heart into her work, a "solutionist", finds answers to problems and thinks of the easiest way to explain these to others, honest, trustworthy, reliable, stable, loyal, visionary, thoughtful, optimistic, one of the best darn networkers.

The first step in developing your personal brand and promoting yourself is to become aware of what makes you unique. You can do part of this work on your own by answering the questions provided in the ***stop and reflect*** sections of this chapter. You may also need to ask others for their opinion as to what differentiates you from the rest of the crowd. This feedback from those who know you well is extremely valuable.

ASKING FOR FEEDBACK

The giving and receiving of ongoing evaluations has now become a significant part of our work lives. In fact, feedback is the foundation of effective leadership and good teamwork.

Being able to ask for and obtain feedback effectively involves communication skills such as managing our emotions, listening actively and asking questions. It also depends on a certain level of trust between the parties involved.

If the thought of asking for feedback makes you uncomfortable, you are not alone. Most of us will have had some experience with receiving an evaluation that was given in an unhelpful way. Because the ability to give effective feedback is so important, many workplaces provide training in communication skills. If your organization doesn't provide these opportunities, the Mindtools website[3] has an excellent Feedback Matrix tool that demonstrates how to ask for advice and also how to make the best use of the information that you receive.

Another excellent place to learn how to give and receive helpful feedback is Toastmasters. Evaluation is built into every Toastmasters meeting as a way of encouraging us learn to become better speakers. But what you may not know is that each and every part of the meeting is reviewed by one of the members. In addition to the speech evaluator there is a general evaluator who reviews the entire meeting and provides valuable feedback to each person in the group. This is done in a friendly and safe environment. In order to facilitate this Toastmasters International provides ongoing education and valuable tools to help members learn how to evaluate effectively.

Getting back to my example at the beginning of this chapter, when I asked people how they perceived me, I chose a few who knew me both personally and through my work. I asked them to participate in the exercise via email which was efficient for all of us because there was no need for individual interviews. It was also a less threatening approach for me than to meet face-to-face. The feedback I received was positive and I believe that it reflects who I am.

Constructive feedback provides us with the opportunity to grow and to make transformational changes in our lives. If you receive unexpected suggestions for improvement you might ask yourself, "Why was I surprised to hear that?" If you receive negative feedback, don't dismiss it out of hand: ask yourself what you can learn from it.

This exercise is not always easy to do but it will lead to you becoming increasingly self-aware. When you are self-aware you are more likely to catch yourself doing something that is not consistent with your true values (which we'll explore in more detail in Chapter Six). As brand strategist Robin Fisher Roffer sums up, "Consistency, clarity, and authenticity are the holy trinity of a great brand."[4]

The most important advice I can give you is to be true to your own values. Despite my reluctance to put myself forward in my professional life, in mid-career I was offered (and accepted) a plum job as an organizational development consultant at a large, acute care hospital in Vancouver. When I asked my boss why I had been chosen for the position, he told me it was because of my integrity. When we act with integrity, we behave in ways that match our values and we strive to be consistent so that people know that they can rely on us. I use the word strive because none of us are perfect. However, when we are aware of what's important to us and how our behaviours are perceived by others, we know that we have developed a solid reputation.

YOUR BRAND IS YOUR REPUTATION

Tom Peters was one of the first leadership experts to write about personal branding. In 1997 he wrote *The Brand Called You* and his advice stands the test of time: " If you are going to be a brand, you've got to become relentlessly focused on what you do that adds value, that you're proud of, and most important, that you can shamelessly take credit for."[5]

Here are some questions to get you started on developing your personal brand:

STOP AND REFLECT

Stop for a moment and reflect on your accomplishments. Don't limit yourself to one aspect of your life.

- WHAT AM I PROUD OF DOING?
- WHAT DO I CONSIDER TO BE MY GREATEST ACCOMPLISHMENTS AND WHY?
- WHAT IS THE MOST EXCITING/IMPORTANT THING I HAVE DONE IN MY LIFE?
- WHAT WOULD OTHERS SAY ARE MY GREATEST ACCOMPLISHMENTS?
- IN WHAT WAYS HAVE I CONTRIBUTED TO MY FAMILY, MY COMMUNITY AND THE ORGANIZATION I WORK FOR?

Once you've taken some time to answer these questions, push yourself to recognize and discuss your successes and accomplishments. Start with people close to you—your friends and family—and then practise at networking meetings and other events.

Branding, a form of marketing, has been used by businesses and not-for-profit organizations for years. It is also a useful tool for individuals and can be particularly beneficial for introverts wanting to raise their profiles.

Author Karley Cunningham debunks the myth that branding is only about marketing. "Branding is less about getting people's attention and more about inviting them to develop a relationship with you."[6] I agree that people will be more likely to want a relationship with you if you promote yourself in a way that honours who you are.

If the idea of branding yourself is still too daunting, consider my own example. I enjoy doing research and finding solutions to problems and I particularly like to share the information I find with people in my network. According to my brand advisors, what I've been doing informally for years has helped me create a brand that works for me.

We all have knowledge, skills and experience that we can share with people in our network. By sharing your expertise in this way it won't be long before you have developed a reputation as the go to person on a particular topic. This kind of approach says a lot about your willingness to help others (image, identity, reputation) at the same time as your profile becomes better known.

Here are some additional questions to help you focus on your strengths and accomplishments:

STOP AND REFLECT

- WHAT DO OTHER PEOPLE SEE AS MY STRENGTHS?
- HOW CAN I CULTIVATE AND DEVELOP THESE STRENGTHS?
- WHAT EXPERTISE AND EXPERIENCE WILL I SHARE WITH THE WORLD?

- WHAT DO I DO BETTER THAN ANYONE ELSE THAT I KNOW?
- WHAT TRAITS AND CHARACTERISTICS ARE MY STRONGEST?
- HOW DO I ADD VALUE?

BE INTENTIONAL ABOUT YOUR PRESENCE

Being the centre of attention can be a scary place for introverts and also a big drain on our energy but as leaders we must be in the spotlight some of the time.

In Chapter Three we focused on how we can manage our energy. Now I want to look at how our energy affects how we are perceived and how we can use this knowledge to project a positive image of ourselves.

The best description of this phenomenon that I've found comes from the work of Patsy Rodenburg, voice coach and author. In *The Second Circle* she identifies three *circles of energy: inward, outward and a balance between the two*.[7]

The *first circle* is the energy of introspection and reflection. These qualities are an important part of whom we are. It's useful too when we don't want to be noticed. I have found myself hiding in this place many times over the course of my career. The danger of spending too much time here is that other people start to overlook us as well, compromising our personal power and effectiveness.

As leaders, we need to be aware of when we are in this state of introspection, because we can unwittingly make people feel "alone, ignored, dismissed and unimportant" as Rodenburg notes.[8] If we need to reflect on something important, we would do better to communicate this to those around us and then spend some time on our own.

In the *third circle* our energy is moving outward and away. This is the place to be when we need to be more assertive or aggressive. This is also a good place to be when we are making a public presentation or wanting to have a strong impact on those who we are trying to influence. But once again, there can be a negative side to taking this approach if there is not a lot of listening is going on and people feel ignored or attacked.

Rodenburg describes the *second circle* as a balanced place. Our energy is focused, not at one extreme or the other, and we enter "the zone" where we feel fully alive. This is the energy of connecting where we both influence others and allow ourselves to be influenced in return.

It's worth working at achieving that balance. One study revealed that about 70% of the population has no inkling of how they appear and interact with others.[9] As a leader, you want to be in the 30% who is seen as being balanced and responsive to the people who are looking to you for direction.

CHARISMA

Many people believe that charisma is the one intangible that differentiates great leaders from others. Indeed, charisma, which is widely associated with extroversion, is often included in job descriptions for leaders.

Not everyone agrees that charisma is the sole preserve of extroverts. Robin Fisher Roffer describes charisma as "a magnetic element of the authentic self and it is something that we are all born with."[10]

What is charisma? I like to think of it as the energy that we create when we are enthusiastic about something and are acting on that passion.

For many of us, becoming more charismatic may feel like a stretch or even an impossibility. At the same time, as leaders, we need to make ourselves visible to other people in our organizations. We can start by reframing charisma as a skill that can be developed, just like other skills needed in today's workplace.

NETWORKING

Networking is another skill that introverts grudgingly accept as a necessary evil for career advancement. Many of us feel ill at ease with the idea of putting ourselves forward in a group setting. Yet everything we do in life, if we want to do it well, is based on developing relationships with other people. This is true of communication, friendship and leadership.

Being an introvert should not stand in the way of our being able to develop genuine relationships. I use the word *genuine* here because I think that a lot of the networking that goes on, especially at formal events, is superficial at best. And if you have little confidence in your social skills, networking, like other leadership skills, is something that will improve the more you practise it.

> "I can really relate to being uncomfortable networking." *Survey Participant*

What, exactly, is networking? Sally Livingston offers this concise description: "a *reciprocal* process based on the *exchange* of ideas, advice, information, referrals, leads, and contacts where resources are *shared* and *acknowledged*."[11]

"It's not what you know but who you know," as the saying goes, and for that reason alone networking is one of the most important skills that we can have in our tool kit. It may surprise you to learn that introverts have the potential to be great networkers because we listen so well to what others have to say.

Today the word network has become part of our language, but for centuries the ability to form close connections with others has been the difference between the success and failure of families, tribes and communities. We rely on our networks of co-workers, family and friends to help us get things accomplished.

Career development professionals have known for a long time that jobs are found through informal networking. Few job opportunities—only 20 per cent by some estimates—are posted in newspapers or even online. One of the most recommended job search techniques is the information interview. By utilizing your network you can gain access to information or actual job leads.

Over the years I have been told that I excel at networking and despite being an introvert I have a large and varied network which keeps growing year by year.

One of the things I instinctively do is to remember specific people whom I meet at conferences, meetings, or social events and I make it a point to stay in touch.

I rarely ask for help for myself but I have put my network to use in the service of others. The interesting thing is that people in my network have remembered me and on occasion approached me with opportunities or leads. Social media such as LinkedIn, Facebook and Twitter, are tools that can extend your reach and make networking easier. These sites enable all of us to keep in touch with people without having to leave our homes or offices.

Recently I had coffee with Steve, a young man who started a MeetUp for introverts interested in leadership. This is what he had to say when I asked him why he decided to start this particular group:

> "When I started my own business I attended a networking event with 100 other people. We were all given a few seconds to introduce ourselves. After that experience, which I didn't find very helpful, I looked around for a smaller group for networking; I couldn't find one so I created it."

Not long after I met with Steve I had coffee with Dave, another introvert who had "taken networking into his own hands". In fact Dave's goal is to be "the most connected individual" in the city where he lives and he is also using MeetUp to help him network with people on a smaller scale.

Sometimes though, you may find yourself attending a larger gathering. When this occurs having an action plan will help reduce your anxiety and ensure you achieve your goals:

1. Make a list of what you want to achieve during your time at the event

2. Stay for 20 minutes to half an hour (of course if you are enjoying yourself you can always stay longer)

3. Strive to meet one or two meaningful connections who you can follow up with in future

4. Manage your energy by taking solo breaks if you feel the need

5. Practice your introduction before you go to the meeting

MENTORS AND COACHES

Mentors are a godsend for introverts. I should know—I have been mentored by a number of great leaders, and, in turn, I have enjoyed mentoring other people. I don't think I ever formally asked anyone to mentor me but I've always been open to receiving advice from managers and senior leaders.

Traditionally, a mentor is someone, usually older and more experienced, who, formally or informally, shares his or her knowledge and experience in order to help us advance in our careers. This definition may be changing, as mentoring author Chelsea Emery points out:

> "In a modern twist mentors are also relying on their protégés. Older employees often depend on younger staff for technology guidance. As employment security wanes, laid-off bosses may need to turn to former subordinates for job leads."[12]

In my career, engaging with mentors was a transformative experience. I was an introvert and loathe to toot my own horn. But the leaders who I worked with saw the potential in me and helped push me out of my comfort zone; they encouraged me to take on new challenges that I would otherwise have missed out on.

If the organization you work for does not have a formal mentoring program and there are no mentors available on an informal basis, then you may have to seek out a mentor on your own. Peer Resources[13] is a Canadian company that provides links to well over 100 mentoring sites around the world and tips for locating a mentor. Some of these resources are general in nature but many focus on special interest groups.

Regardless of whether you search for an advisor in person or over the internet, remember that seeking out a mentor is an *intentional* act. It means that you are taking charge of your career and your success in life.

GET OVER YOUR FEAR OF SUCCESS

Many of us—introverts and extroverts alike—fear success. But introverts may be more prone to ruminating instead of moving on and taking action. Understanding what success means to you and becoming more comfortable with the idea of being successful is an important first step and one that can be facilitated by asking yourself the following questions:

STOP AND REFLECT

- WHERE HAVE I ACHIEVED MY GREATEST SUCCESS IN LIFE?
- WHAT DOES SUCCESS MEAN TO ME?
- WHAT MIGHT GET IN THE WAY OF MY ACHIEVING SUCCESS AS I DEFINE IT?
- HOW DO I CELEBRATE MY SUCCESSES NOW?
- HOW COULD I CELEBRATE MY SUCCESSES IN FUTURE?

On a recent visit to my close friend Norma, I browsed through her extensive library and came across Cheryl Richardson's book *Stand Up for Your Life*.[14] I was immediately attracted to the title which sounded as if it could be the introvert's motto. "Owning our talents and gifts can feel like a risky proposition," writes Richardson.

But this is what we must do if we want to have a rewarding career—and personal branding is all about identifying the qualities that are uniquely ours and sharing them with the world.

How has being an introvert affected your career both positively and negatively? The last word in this chapter goes to one of my survey participants who responded to this question.

"Negative—lack of willingness to 'self-market'. Positive—I enjoy facilitating group work, am a good listener; want to find out about the people I'm interacting with—being an introvert enables/compels me to get over my anxieties about impressing others and to interface with new people, situations, work environments; I usually feel good about the process once it's completed." *Survey Participant*

CHAPTER SUMMARY

- Over the years introversion has become associated with a number of negative traits such as passivity, reclusiveness and self-centeredness.

- Introverts can learn how to promote the many positive attributes that they possess.

- We will feel more at ease promoting ourselves if we can find ways to promote ourselves that represent who we are.

- Asking for feedback from people we trust in order to become more self-aware is a sign of a strong leader.

- Networking is a necessary skill for developing both personal and business relationships.

CHAPTER FIVE
The Introverted Leader Advantage

"THE MORE WE UNDERSTAND EACH OTHER THE
MORE WE CAN CREATE A POSITIVE AND PRODUCTIVE
ENVIRONMENT FOR US ALL."[1]
Mike Johnson

Why should organizations recognize, develop and promote introverts? The short answer is because it is in their best interest to do so. You don't have to look very far to see that private sector businesses and non-profits alike are looking for every advantage they can find to help them stay competitive in today's economy. I have argued throughout this book that introverts have dynamism of their own to offer. Like extroverts, they are potential sources of expertise and wisdom and it is time for organizations to recognize this fact.

In his 2002 bestseller, *Good to Great*, Jim Collins popularized the idea of "getting the right people on the bus."[2] He was referring to an organization's mandate to hire employees with the right combination of skills, attitude, experience and knowledge. And while Collins was not thinking about personality types specifically, his findings support the need for a quiet leader, one who listens and creates opportunities for others to contribute their ideas. Introverts are ideal candidates for this leadership model; they present a hidden advantage in winning the "war for talent".

The term "war for talent" was coined by Steven Hankin of McKinsey & Company in 1997.[3] Organizations have bought into this concept and are constantly on the lookout for ammunition that will give them the edge. Unfortunately, rather than recognizing the benefits of hiring people with different leadership styles, in recent years this ammunition has taken the form of personality tests. Rodney Warrenfeltz has written that this is "one of the fastest growing trends in the field of human resources."[4] In some instances, these tests are being used to screen out introverts.

If, as I believe, no one size fits all when it comes to the type of leadership that organizations need, it is regrettable that many employers are not aware of the contributions that introverts make. According to Adam Grant, a management professor at the Wharton School of Business, University of Pennsylvania, introverts are excellent candidates for leadership in today's organizations.

> *"I think the introverted leader advantage is growing because the need for employee proactivity is growing. Organizations have become flatter, and work has become more dynamic and unpredictable, so we rely more heavily on proactive employees to take initiative and create change from the bottom up. As you know from our studies, introverted leaders tend to be highly effective when paired with proactive employees."*[5]

LEADING ENGAGED EMPLOYEES

There is considerable research demonstrating the benefits of hiring and supporting proactive workers and I believe that Adam Grant's research on the effectiveness of introverted leaders provides us with another way of thinking about employee engagement. Organizations need proactive employees; however, a 2011 Gallup study found that the majority of Americans (71%) were either not engaged or actively disengaged in their work.[6]

What do we mean by employee engagement? Engaged employees go above and beyond what is written in their job descriptions. They perform above expectation because they want to contribute and because it is in the best interest of their employer. This is known as discretionary effort or discretionary energy.

An employee's desire to contribute is the key for innovative organizations needing to continually improve products and services. It seems that discretionary energy is also an important ingredient in keeping clients and customers happy.

Organizations spend millions of dollars each year in North America to recruit, train and retain employees. Why then are so many of us disengaged? Why do so few of our current leaders show us how we can be factors in our organization's vision of the future? Perhaps we are not inspired to do our best work because we don't feel connected to the values of the organizations we work for. The latter may, in my view, be the case for introverts working in organizations that favour extroverts. Perhaps we feel our ideas aren't taken seriously. If employers want to engage us they need to recognize that introverts and extroverts express their ideas differently.

RESPECTING A VARIETY OF COMMUNICATION STYLES

Given our personality differences it should come as no surprise that introverts and extroverts have different communication styles. Extroverts tend to talk more often, more quickly and with more self-assuredness while introverts listen more than they speak and may appear tentative and less confident.

> "The 'negative' impacts seem to outweigh the benefits in terms of the sweeping perceptions of others that I was too quiet, and or didn't speak with the kind of 'authority' that seemed to be required of leaders, i.e. I often asked questions rather than speak declaratively, which is what often seems to confer credibility… I found myself struggling in an environment where the mere capacity to talk, talk, talk was more persuasive to others than the capacity to listen." *Survey Participant*
>
> •
>
> "Managers need to pay attention to all their staff—not just the ones who make noise." *Survey Participant.*

Organizational culture refers to the unwritten rules that dictate how things work and what is valued in the organization, e g "the way things are done around here". An organization's culture is continually reinforced through the stories that are told, and in the past decade, storytelling has become a popular communications tool used by leaders. Using images to capture people's imaginations helps us remember the message longer than simply stating facts and figures.

Storytelling is also one of the primary ways that we learn about what is important in the organizations we work for. If all stories tend to be about leaders who are undeniably extroverted, then the messages may have the unintended consequence of turning off introverted employees.

> "Start telling different stories about how people should be. Not everybody enjoys or takes advantage of learning or working in groups, some of us are actually much more productive alone, and people can even block our productivity and creativity." *Survey Participant*

By telling different stories we can begin to demonstrate that both introverted and extroverted behaviours are valued.

THE INVISIBLE MAJORITY – SUPPORTING A BROADER DEFINITION OF DIVERSITY

The importance of diversity in the workplace has long been recognized and great strides have been made over the past few decades. Diversity training in organizations typically takes into consideration the following differences among people: gender, culture, ethnicity, age, religion/spirituality, class, and physical and mental abilities.

Although introverts make up half of the workforce, we may feel invisible at times especially when we are overlooked for promotion or our ideas are not listened to.

We don't usually think about including introversion in diversity programs because introverts are not seen as needing special accommodation in the workplace. But according to blogger Andy Johnson, "Introversion is a facet, perhaps one of the most powerful, of diversity."[7] But how many organizations recognize that introverts, as a group, may be marginalized or devalued? If the goal of diversity programs is to create workplaces that are inclusive and promote teamwork, employee engagement, acceptance of differences and avoidance of conflict, it follows that promoting an understanding of both introversion and extroversion is necessary.

> "Leaders and management should promote understanding, and acceptance of the different personalities, cultural backgrounds, and generational differences in the workforce and society at large. Encouragement and acceptance of our differences will create better situations for everyone, and will result in more and better opinions, suggestions, and procedures for the organizations themselves." *Survey Participant*

AWARENESS AND EDUCATION ARE KEY

One recurring theme that emerged from my survey on leadership and introversion is the need for awareness and education. People often make incorrect assumptions about introverts because they have little or no information to base their judgments on. As we've seen, introverts are often assumed to be shy or lacking in confidence because they are slower to speak up and take longer to process information and make decisions.

The flip side is that because introverts take longer to consider information they may make better decisions.

> "…in my experience the lack of knowledge or ignorance of introversion is the biggest challenge to overcome…awareness is the key." *Survey Participant*

> "Become educated about what an introvert actually is (as opposed to the many misconceptions out there). Learn to appreciate the many different styles that people have and work to play on people's strengths as opposed to wanting everyone to conform to one way of doing things. Use people's areas of strength when assigning them for committees, projects etc." *Survey Participant*

How do we go about increasing awareness and education of differences at all levels of the organization? A popular approach to helping employees understand each other is through the use of personality tests such as the Myers Briggs Type Indicator (MBTI). The MBTI is loosely based on Carl Jung's theory of psychological type and can be a useful tool to understand how we perceive the world and how we make decisions based on our preferences.

However, the way in which testing is conducted is critical. Patricia Cranton, an adult educator, cautions that the traditional approaches to using personality testing may only reinforce labels and stereotypes if there is no opportunity for dialogue.[8] If my own experience is any indicator, then I agree with the need to rethink how we use personality tests in our organizations.

I have had to complete the MBTI on more than one occasion as part of a team building process or retreat. To my knowledge, completing the questionnaire was the primary focus. There was little or no feedback about what our results meant to ourselves or to the team. Consequently the exercise was quickly forgotten.

Some organizations go so far as to have all employees complete the MBTI and wear their results on their name tags. (Hi, I'm INTJ or Hi, I'm ENSP). This awareness on its own does not go far enough in helping us to understand our differences and—if not handled with sensitivity—can end up reinforcing negative stereotypes about the different personality types.

Worse, if not facilitated properly, these exercises can backfire as demonstrated by the following example from Vanessa, an educator and self-described introvert:

> *"After doing a survey as to whether we were introverts or extroverts, we were divided into those two groups and told to come up with a list of what it was like dealing with the other group. We introverts went first, and talked about things like needing time away from the social or interactive scene which didn't always mesh with what the extroverts wanted from us. Then the extroverts talked about what it was like to work with us introverts. They produced a litany of complaints about how annoying it was to always have to stop and coax us to participate, and how tired they were of having to pay attention to our feelings—why didn't we just step up to the plate—and on and on....I felt attacked for being who I was, my very essence, and I could not believe that the facilitator didn't step in to redress the imbalance at the end. But no....the workshop just moved on... (I should have talked to the facilitator, but I didn't—I was too emotional about it)."*[9]

When I asked Vanessa for permission to quote her, she replied, *"I would like the message to get out there—it was a prime example of being in a minority and treated as marginal."*

Unfortunately this is not an isolated case. Organizations spend significant amounts of money paying for workshops that are not part of an integrated diversity program and end up doing more harm than good. While open, honest communication may be the goal, this is only possible if we have developed relationships with the people we are working with and that these relationships are based on a foundation of trust.

MINDSETS

Organizations, like people, have different ways of viewing the world. These world views are powerful, yet often go unnoticed unless someone challenges them. Even then it takes a long time for change to happen. In *Mindset*, author Carol Dweck describes two belief systems that she identified in her research at Stanford University: the *fixed* mindset and the *flexible* mindset.[10]

For most of the 20th century it was widely believed that those who exhibited extroverted behaviours were better leaders.

This is one example of how a fixed mindset can hurt an organization. Mistaken beliefs about the lack of leadership potential of introverts is another example of the negative effects of a fixed mindset—one that hurts both the organization and the individual.

Organizations lose a source of much needed leadership talent when introverts are overlooked and introverts themselves find that their careers have stalled. An article on the University of Kansas website summarizes this well: "When we think about whom to train for leadership, it's easy to overlook people who don't fit our stereotypical image of a *leader*...we often don't consider quiet or shy individuals to be potential leaders".[11]

If we want to engage introverts we need to plan strategically, but it will take a collective shift in our perceptions of leaders and leadership. Let's consider what a more balanced and inclusive approach to leadership could look like and how our organizations can make this a reality. Here are some questions to get started:

STOP & REFLECT

- HOW IS LEADERSHIP RECOGNIZED IN MY ORGANIZATION?
- WHERE IS LEADERSHIP NEEDED IN THE ORGANIZATION NOW AND IN THE FUTURE?
- WHAT KINDS OF KNOWLEDGE, SKILLS AND EXPERIENCE WILL THESE LEADERS HAVE?
- WILL LEADERSHIP BE DEVELOPED FROM WITHIN THE ORGANIZATION OR RECRUITED FROM OUTSIDE?
- IF DEVELOPED FROM WITHIN, HOW WILL LEADERS BE DEVELOPED?

A story in *Business in Vancouver* highlights how a CEO's ability to listen impacts an organization's bottom line positively. David Schellenberg, winner of the 2012 British Columbia CEO award, has pinpointed that "...you really need to be a great listener." His leadership style demonstrates the value of thoughtful decision-making. As a result Conair Group Inc. is growing, his employees are engaged and there is virtually no turnover.[12]

"Wait and listen. Speak to them alone, don't assume that they are not contributing or are not able to contribute. Encourage them to take risks around career and guarantee a safety net so they can do it." *Survey Participant*

THE ROLE OF HUMAN RESOURCES

The most effective workplaces will strive to have a balance of introverts and extroverts. In order to achieve this goal your organization may need to rethink some of its human resources policies and procedures such as recruitment, onboarding, leadership development, team building, and diversity.

THE RECRUITING PROCESS

"How about sending the job interview questions out before the interview?" asked Susanne during one of our many discussions about introversion. "We can't do that!" was my immediate reaction. "Why not?" responded Susanne. Why not indeed?

The first step in engaging introverts may actually be before they become employees. You want to hire the right person for the job and since half of the population is introverted you might want to think about revising your hiring process. Start by asking the following questions:

STOP & REFLECT

- WHAT COULD OUR ORGANIZATION DO DIFFERENTLY?
- HOW WOULD WE WORD OUR ADS AND JOB DESCRIPTIONS SO THAT THEY ARE INCLUSIVE OF INTROVERTS?
- WHAT WOULD THE INTERVIEW PROCESS LOOK LIKE?
- HOW CAN THIS PROCESS BE MADE TO BE PERSONAL AND UNIQUE FOR EACH PERSON?

On its website the Vancity Credit Union[13] offers job seekers advice on how to prepare for an interview. Although not specifically targeted toward introverts this type of information helps all job candidates feel more in charge of the interview process.

As organizations compete for the best possible talent, everyone benefits by becoming more creative and innovative in their hiring practices. Currently, extroverts seem to have the edge when it comes to job interviews. In order to be fair to everyone, it's in the employer's best interest to create interview scenarios that showcase an introvert's strengths such as problem-solving and analytical thinking.

In most situations, it will be impossible for employers to know beforehand if someone is an introvert, so it is up to both the employer and the job seeker to ensure that introverts are given the same opportunity as extroverts who are applying for the same job:

- Introverts can self-disclose as soon as they have been offered an interview

- Employers can take the needs of introverts into consideration and modify the interview process using some of the suggestions in this book.

As awareness of these issues grows, it will be easier for introverts to speak up and ask for what they need when applying for work.

Typically, job interviews are conducted in one of three ways: one-to-one, panel or group. All of these interviews provide an opportunity for both the employer and the job applicant to gain more information. The employer will have a set of prepared questions to ask. The job candidate should also come prepared to ask questions about the organization and the particular job opportunity.

Nowadays interviews are also conducted using SKYPE (a computer software program that allows users to connect with other people using voice and live images). This technology is being used to allow people in different locations to interview job candidates as a team. Rather than having to participate in a live panel interview this technology can level the playing field for introverts who may not do their best when being asked to answer questions quickly in a group.

Panel interviews involve the job candidate being interviewed by two or more people at the same time. These are often used because they are considered an efficient use of the interviewers' time but they can be intimidating. "Having an extrovert waiting to get called into an interview in a crowded reception area might be energizing while an introvert may be unable to concentrate. Options for quiet spaces to wait might be a good idea." writes Relationship Coach Rosalie Boulter.[14]

A variation on the panel interview is the group interview which can be even more alarming for introverts. Group interviews often include all of the candidates for a job plus the interviewers and even recruiters. If a group interview is necessary for your organization, consider providing the questions ahead of time.

As an introvert, you will have to push yourself out of your comfort zone in order to ace a group interview. You will be required to introduce yourself to the entire group which could include the employer and other potential candidates. Because one of the objectives of a group interview, from the employer's perspective, is to see how you interact with others, you will be expected to talk to the other people in the room.

Information overload is common during a job interview. In order to reduce the impact of having too much information and not enough time to process it, introverts need to assert themselves by asking for questions and other information requests to be made available in writing.

THE ONBOARDING PROCESS

Once an employee has been hired, organizations need to think about the onboarding process. Onboarding is a human resources term to describe the process of orienting, socializing, and training new employees. Successful onboarding has been linked to employee engagement and retention. This process may last for up to a year but the first few weeks are the most intense, filled with meet and greets, formal orientation sessions and training. If not managed well, this period could lead to overload for introverts. Suggestions for accommodating introverts include: using a buddy system, recognizing the need for downtime, and providing quiet space.

A Google search identified a number of comprehensive onboarding programs offered by organizations. I felt overwhelmed just reading about them. I couldn't imagine how a new introverted leader would cope so I contacted Stacy Doepner who had developed such a program for the University of Minnesota. I asked her if she had considered the needs of introverts in her design. While the program initially focussed on generalizations, related Doepner-Hove, as it progressed "we had begun to think about how we would adjust [it] to many different learning and personality types."[15]

PERFORMANCE REVIEWS

I have never liked being asked to participate in a performance review and I suspect that a lot of you may have similar feelings.

Is it the way in which we are given feedback? The purpose of a performance review is not a one-way communication from your boss to you; it is about having a conversation about how you are doing and what you need in order to achieve your performance goals (e g, resources, training, coaching). It begins with a good relationship, based on trust and respect.

Ideally, feedback on one's performance should occur on an ongoing basis. In 1982, Tom Peters and Robert Waterman popularized the term "management by walking around" in their book *In Search of Excellence*.[16] This type of leadership recognizes the importance of checking in with people to recognize them for the positive things that they are doing or to help them if they are struggling. I remember being told that one should never receive any surprises during a formal performance review, such as "you've not been doing your job as expected and this will now be part of your permanent record."

Good leaders provide feedback on a regular basis. This informal feedback is much more valuable than the formal feedback that most of us are accustomed to receiving once a year. By letting people know how their work is playing a role, leaders are helping to shape the culture of the organization in positive ways.

> "Create expanded performance metrics to recognize the value introverts bring to the workplace." *Survey Participant*

Additional resources about performance reviews can be found at the HR Council, a Canadian human resources organization.[17]

ENCOURAGING INTROVERTS TO DO THEIR BEST WORK

"Are we making a mistake by requiring introverts to participate in teamwork?" asks Michael Haberman, senior consultant with Omega HR Solutions.[18] To this provocative question, I would add: "How can we reframe the way we work together so that both introverts and extroverts can contribute to the best of their abilities and feel that they are engaged?"

> "Have supervisors who are trained to recognize the traits of introverts and who are experts in ways to include everyone in the discussions/planning and give adequate time to everyone in the group. If you are lucky enough to have a supervisor like that you know what I mean." *Survey Participant*

In Chapter Three I highlighted the importance of creating environments—the structures, systems and processes—that encourage introverts to do their best work. In addition to creating optimal environments for individuals to work on their own, let's consider the type of team environments (also known as team climate or culture) that are being created. Depending on your job, the type of industry (e.g. health care, technology, education, finance or construction) and the organization you work for, you will most likely spend some of your time working within a group.

When they are working well together, teams of people with different skills and areas of expertise can positively impact the organization's bottom line by creatively solving problems, completing projects and identifying ideas for new products and services. But despite the promise that teams can do great things and the financial resources spent on developing and supporting them, many teams fail to live up to expectations.

You only need to watch a mixed group of introverts and extroverts to know that they communicate differently. In general introverts need to think before they talk and extroverts think and talk at the same time. Communication could be a recipe for disaster if team members are not aware of their differences and don't know how to accommodate them.

In his *Manual for Working with Teams*, Steve Borgatti identifies the challenges faced by the team when introverted members are not supported:

> *"When team members disappear, it is not entirely their fault. It is your fault too. Take someone who is introverted. They find it stressful to talk in a group. They like to think things through before they start talking. They consider others' feelings and don't want to tell them when they are wrong. In a group full of extroverts, this person cannot find a way to participate: it is not in their nature to fight for attention. It is the extroverts' responsibility to consciously include the introvert, to not talk over them, to not take the floor away from them."*[19]

Why is it that some of us remain silent while participating in meetings or other group activities only to become non-stop motor-mouths once the meeting is over? I have observed this behaviour during my time working in healthcare. I often thought it was strange that many of the leaders, who had not spoken up when they had the opportunity, would congregate in the hallway after the meeting and voice their opinions about what had just occurred. Looking back, I suspect that if these meetings had been designed to help people find their voices within the group, there would have been less need to spend so much time meeting in the hallway.

Successful teamwork takes time, commitment and the right skills. Diverse teams can be an asset when team members recognize and respect each other's differences and learn how to work together toward a common goal.

But even within these teams, most people need time to quietly reflect on their work. This is especially important when we get stuck and run out of ideas. How many of us have gone for a walk while pondering a difficult problem and had an "aha" moment when a solution popped into our head? Effective teams will build in time during meetings (or immediately before or afterwards) for this type of reflection.

Here are a few examples of group techniques, activities and exercises designed to allow people time to pause before they speak or to work on their own during team meetings:

- a talking stick* so that only one person at a time is allowed to speak

- ground rules** for participation

- silent brainstorming, a technique that allows individuals to generate ideas on their own and then discuss as a group.

Other examples of group techniques can be found on the Mindtools website.[20]

---

* A talking stick is tool used to help facilitate communication. It was originally used by First Nations during council meetings. Whoever held the stick had the total attention of the group. Nowadays the talking stick is used by a variety of groups and has found its way into the corporate world. It ensures that each person has a turn to speak without being interrupted and encourages everyone to listen more carefully to the ideas that are being presented.

** Ground rules are agreed upon expectations of how a group will work together. They ensure that everyone has the opportunity to participate. Examples include: listening attentively, building on one another's comments, and sharing responsibility for the success of the group. Ground rules should be agreed upon when the group first begins its work together.

In addition to being creative in how you approach meetings and group work, clarifying the roles and expectations of participants will lead to more effective meetings. Next time you are facilitating a meeting or are asked to join a new group use the following questions to get everyone started on the "right foot":

1. When I was asked to join this group I understood my role was...

2. I was asked to serve on this committee because...

3. Before I joined this group I wish someone would have told me...

4. I would feel more effective as a group member if...

5. To improve our effectiveness as a group I think we should...

We know that far too often introverted qualities such as listening, reflection, critical thinking and solitude are undervalued. We also know that misunderstanding can lead to conflict, so team leaders need to know why introverts in their organizations behave the way they do (e.g. take time to process information). Teams will also want to look at ways of benefiting from including the contributions of both introverts and extroverts. Here are some questions to get you thinking about balancing your teams:

STOP & REFLECT

- WHAT DO INTROVERTS (AND EXTROVERTS) BRING TO THE TEAM?
- WHAT TOOLS, TECHNIQUES, AND PROCESSES CAN WE USE TO HELP INTROVERTS PARTICIPATE?
- WHAT DO INTROVERTED TEAM MEMBERS NEED?
- HOW CAN WE USE TECHNOLOGY TO FACILITATE TEAMWORK?
- WHEN IS THE BEST TIME TO PUT AN INTROVERT IN CHARGE OF THE TEAM?

These questions can be used as part of an overall review of teams in your organization or they can be used with individual teams as part of teaming. In that case you might want to rephrase the questions to ask what all team members bring to the team and what they need in order to do their best work.

"Set up an maintain an organizational structure and culture that favours teamwork/collaboration over competition, relies on people interacting in small working groups or "pods" whenever possible, and promotes strong, consistent and open lines of communication."
Survey Participant

MENTORING AND COACHING

Because many introverts prefer to work on their own, they may not get the help they need in order to advance in their careers. Working with a mentor will provide introverted employees with the opportunity to meet people they might otherwise not come into contact with. Mentors offer advice, share their knowledge and experience and can help employees to develop new skills. They may also be a source of emotional support.

Formal mentors can be assigned to you as part of your organization's mentoring program, while informal mentors are people who voluntarily choose to assist you with your career. I have been fortunate to have had a number of informal mentors. My mentors were all older than me and in more senior positions. They had observed that I was interested in learning: taking courses, reading and when the opportunity arose, teaching and helping others.

> "Do introverts know who they are—their challenges and strengths? I suppose organizations need to develop tools—or mentorship programs—for all personality / leadership types to understand themselves and others. Such an organization would change the language used and be promoting healthy communication and acceptance for a broad range of human expression. This means that within the organization employees take responsibility for themselves as well as develop their relational skills with others." *Survey Participant*

Mentoring and coaching can be valuable for introverts during their onboarding process and at other transitions during employment. What's the difference between the two approaches? Mentoring involves having someone else share their experience and expertise with you, while coaching, in the form of questions and answers, assumes that you are the expert. In many organizations it is not unusual for both mentoring and coaching to be used.

Jane, a self-described introvert, works closely with another leader who is an extrovert. "The two of us make a good team and often joke that together we would make the perfect clinical coordinator," she told me. Jane added that her success as a leader is due in part to the fact that she has someone to role-play tough situations with. "Don't let being an introvert stop you from applying for a leadership position," she concluded. "Take courses, read, and have someone to bounce things off."

In addition to the suggestions made above, mentors and coaches can also be enlisted to help with the following challenges:

- Developing your leadership skills and abilities
- Understanding and dealing with a conflict situation
- Navigating organizational politics
- Exploring work-life balance and reducing stress

THE HIDDEN COSTS OF IGNORING INTROVERTS

Workplace stress is costing Canadian organizations billions of dollars a year in lost productivity and sick time. A 2008 study by Partners for Mental Health found that ignoring mental health issues such as stress, anxiety, and depression drains the Canadian economy by $51 billion each year.[21] And a recent Mindtools blog post on the topic of burnout noted that job stress is costing US industry $300 billion dollars a year. [22]

> "Energy is definitely affected as I go home exhausted and not wanting to interact with my family." *Survey Participant*

It seems to me that there is a fundamental contradiction in our organizations: we value extroverted leaders by recognizing and promoting them for their high energy and charisma. At the same time, our workplaces are on overdrive and struggling to deal with burnout, stress-related illnesses and decreased productivity.

A majority of the respondents in the Leadership and Introversion Survey that I conducted identified stress and low energy as negative factors in their careers. However, these leaders showed tremendous resilience by recognizing their stress and learning how to slow down and manage it.

WHAT CAN ORGANIZATIONS DO TO ADDRESS THIS ISSUE?

Organizations can begin to address this issue by learning to listen to what employees need in order to effectively manage stress. This is where introverts can provide leadership. Remember that we are, by necessity, experts on finding ways to reduce our anxiety and stress levels.

CHAPTER SUMMARY

- Organizations need every advantage if they want to succeed and this includes rethinking the unique attributes and skills introverts contribute as leaders.

- The introverted leader advantage gives organizations the edge in the war for talent.

- In order to hire and promote introverts, organizations may have to revamp their human resource policies in the areas of recruitment, hiring, onboarding, performance reviews, and promotion.

- Diversity programs need to be expanded to help employees understand and accept the characteristics of the different personality types.

- Teams become more creative and productive when everyone's voice is heard.

- Awareness and education is required to counteract the assumptions and misconceptions that people have about introverts and introversion.

CHAPTER SIX
Your Personal Leadership Development Plan

"IT'S PROBABLY A BETTER TIME TO BE AN INTROVERTED LEADER
NOW THAN AT ANY PREVIOUS TIME ON RECORD."
Adam Grant, 2011[i]

Planning prepares us to take advantage of opportunities as they arise. If Adam Grant is correct, and I believe that he is, the world is waking up to the advantages of being an introvert—seeing introversion as a positive force in the world.

There are many definitions of leadership. Enlisting others in achieving a common goal is one that is short and to the point. The goal can be as small as a group of friends preparing dinner together or as large as being in charge of planning an international conference or starting a new business.

I believe that we all have leadership potential and that we are all called on to lead at various times in our lives. Some of us will actively seek out formal leadership positions at work and in our communities. Introverts like myself, may be content to quietly wait to be recognized and given the opportunity to lead. Whatever your style, remember that few people, be they are extroverted or introverted, are born leaders. Bill

George, author of *Authentic Leadership*,[2] argues that we have to develop ourselves in order to mature into good leaders.

This chapter will provide further opportunities for you to reflect on your current leadership style and skills. By determining what kind of leader you are now, by assessing your ability to lead, by learning new skills and by challenging yourself to lead more effectively, you will make great strides toward achieving your leadership goals.

When I first decided to leave my front line position and move forward in my career, I set my sights on leading a small team of public health professionals. I realized I needed some training in leading others and I signed up for as many courses as I could that were offered by my employer. It was a common practice in those days for managers to be "back-filled" when they went on vacation; recognizing this fact, I asked my boss for the opportunity to substitute for her. It wasn't long before an opening presented itself. I was ready—or as ready as I could be—for the challenge.

In their book, *The Leadership Challenge*, authors Kouzes and Posner give us another reason to plan. "Proactive people tend to work harder at what they do. They achieve their goals when others give up."[3] Introverts may be well-represented in this group, if the comments of some of the leaders who completed my online survey are any example.

"Overall, I haven't noticed introversion as a major barrier in my career, but it has required me to perhaps work harder at things that might otherwise have been accomplished with relative ease." *Survey Participant*

One tool I have found helpful is a personal leadership development plan (PLDP). The design is not a new one and students in leadership development programs will be familiar with the concept. In this chapter I make suggestions for what to include in your plan. In the end, however, your plan will be as individual as you are.

WHAT IS A PERSONAL LEADERSHIP DEVELOPMENT PLAN?

A personal leadership development plan is a place for you to discover who you are, where you have been and where you are going. You can use your PLDP to explore your beliefs, values, interests, life experiences and your personality and character traits. You will be more successful if you can tap into your passion and purpose by aligning your values and beliefs with your goals.

There is no right or wrong way to develop your PLDP but you do need to put your own stamp on it. Leadership expert Daniel Goleman argues that "if you try and follow a "prescribed model, you may find that it doesn't work for you."[4] However, certain elements are common to most PLDPs. They include:

- Vision, purpose and values
- Personality traits
- Strengths and areas for improvement
- Goals and action plans
- Legacy

Although we can't predict what lies ahead, we can all imagine the type of future that we would like to live in.

To be truly powerful our visions should include what we want for our life as a whole and not just for our work. They should excite and challenge us and we must believe we are capable of realizing them. Creating a vision that integrates our sense of purpose and our values will motivate us to achieve our goals.

There are a number of interesting approaches that you can use to create your vision of the future. One is the use of a journal to capture your ideas in writing and images or an electronic device to record them digitally. Regardless of what medium you choose, remember to return to it from time to time. It can be a powerful reminder of what you plan to achieve in life.

WHAT IS A VISION BOARD?

One popular way of working on a personal vision, inspired by *The Secret*, is a vision board.[5] You will need a poster board, magazines or photographs, scissors, and tape or paste. Go through magazines and newspapers and cut out pictures or words that appeal to your vision and attach them to your board. Once you have chosen pictures that inspire you (including one of yourself), attach them to the poster board.

PURPOSE

We all have a life purpose. In Chapter Three we looked at how life purpose impacts our personal energy and why it is an especially important tool for introverts. Knowing who we are and what we are meant to be doing with our lives provides a strong source of personal energy.

One of the most accessible ways to get clear on your purpose is to ask yourself a series of questions. Here are a few to get you started:

STOP & REFLECT

- WHAT AM I GOOD AT?
- IF I WERE TO TEACH A CLASS, WHAT WOULD I TEACH?
- IF I COULD MAKE A DIFFERENCE IN THE WORLD WHAT WOULD I DO?
- WHAT ACTIVITIES MAKE ME LOSE TRACK OF TIME?
- WHEN I'M WORKING ON SOMETHING THAT I'M NOT INTERESTED IN, WHAT DO I FIND MYSELF DAYDREAMING ABOUT?
- AT THE END OF MY LIFE WHAT DO I WANT TO BE REMEMBERED FOR?
- WHAT ARE MY NATURAL TALENTS? WHAT DO I DO EASILY THAT I DON'T HAVE TO THINK ABOUT?

Other clues may come from how your friends, family and colleagues see you.

Ultimately, we need to look within ourselves to find the answers to these age old questions.

A few years ago I found myself working at a job that wasn't a fit for me. Although the work was easy, and paid well, I knew it wasn't what I was meant to be doing. I was often bored and found myself dreaming about doing other things with my life.

My circumstances changed suddenly when my boss left the organization. I found myself in a position to work for myself which gave me the flexibility to begin writing professionally.

DEVELOPING OUR PERSONALITIES

A common belief in the past held that our personalities were fixed. According to that viewpoint, we are born with certain traits and these traits stay pretty much the same throughout our lives. We now know that "we can consciously develop our personalities by setting goals for our personality development."[6] But the idea of changing ourselves in this way is not without its detractors. Some argue that there is nothing wrong with being an introvert and that we should be recognized for our introverted qualities and celebrated for who we are. I agree that we should celebrate our introversion but also recognize that in order to succeed in life we need to be flexible and able to adapt to what life throws our way.

This ability to adapt to the circumstances that we find ourselves in is a crucial quality of effective leaders. Situational leadership[7] dictates that we "flex" our behaviours to suit the circumstances, regardless of whether we are introverts or extroverts. So, quiet introverts may need to speak loudly when the situation calls for it. By contrast, extroverts may need to learn to listen instead of talk.

This flexing may not be as difficult as it looks. "Although we generally have a preference for introversion or extraversion, we are likely able to function in both," writes adult educator Patricia Cranton.[8] If you think of introversion or extroversion as a continuum, most of us are able to move between the two poles depending on the demands of the situation.

So, how do we go about changing our personalities? How do we go about becoming more comfortable with skills traditionally associated with extroversion?

The first step is to become aware of how we are behaving and what behaviours we need or want to change. In my own case, it was the self-awareness that I must overcome my fear of speaking in public that led me to confront my fears.

If you want to discover how you are perceived by others, one of the best ways is to start by asking people you trust for some constructive feedback. In Chapter Four, we looked at this approach in our discussion of personal branding.

Large organizations often use a process called a 360 degree evaluation[9] as a means of helping employees identify their strengths and areas for improvement. If your employer doesn't provide you with this type of developmental opportunity and you'd like to give this a try, you will be asking for feedback from the people who report to you, your peers and colleagues, and from the person to whom you report. You may want to consider asking your clients or customers for feedback if this is appropriate. This process can feel risky, so you should have some say into who gives you the feedback.

There are also a sizable number of tests that can enlighten us about our personality, conflict communication style, emotional intelligence (EQ), and resilience (RQ). Many of these tools are available on the internet. If you work in an organization that supports you as a leader, it may cover costs for tests that it deems valuable for your professional development.

You may also consider working with someone to help you make sense of what you are learning about yourself: coaches and mentors can play a role here.

The research on leadership and leadership development shows that the most effective leaders are those who understand their own personalities and the personalities of the people around them.

VALUES

Values are both universal and individual. Universal values such as a striving for love, peace and family are shared around the world. At the same time, we also have values that are unique to our own selves.

Values express what matters to us. When we clarify our values we can set goals and focus on that which is important to us. Indeed, when we attempt to do things that are not in line with our values we will find that we have less energy.

Being clear on what our values are will be of benefit when we are faced with difficult decisions. In fact, people admire those of us who believe in something strongly and are willing to stand up for our beliefs.

There are numerous ways to help us to identify and explore our values. Here are a few suggestions.

STOP & REFLECT

Identify specific moments in your life when life was especially rewarding for you and reflect on the following questions:

- What was important about this moment?
- What values was I living in this moment?

Here are some other questions to help you to reflect on what your values are:

- Who am I at my very best?
- What qualities do I want in a friend or a partner?
- What must I have in my life to be fulfilled?

Once you have identified your values, ask yourself how your values show up in your life.

STRENGTHS AND AREAS FOR IMPROVEMENT

Your strengths and areas for improvement can be captured in your personal SWOT which stands for:

S   personal **strengths** that you can build on
W   personal **weaknesses** or areas for **improvement**
O   **opportunities** present in your workplace or in the wider community
T   **threats** which include changes in your organization or industry that might impact your job or your career

Also known as a SWOT analysis, this tool was originally developed for the business leader who wanted to understand how his or her company compared to its competitors. Today the SWOT is increasingly being used as a personal planning tool.

As a dynamic introvert, your strengths may include your ability to manage projects with sensitivity, handle conflict and take the time needed to make good decisions.

Your areas for improvement may include promoting yourself by speaking up at work or managing your energy.

You can use the information that you glean from completing a SWOT to support your vision or to identify new goals and to create an action plan to help you achieve these goals.

GOAL SETTING & ACTION PLANS

It seems like I've always been setting goals for myself. However, not everyone sees the benefit of doing this type of work. Many years ago a friend revealed that he would become so focused on achieving his goals that he would miss out on other opportunities that presented themselves. Dennis equated goal setting with a loss of spontaneity. Over the years I've learned that it is possible to set both short and long term goals and at the same time remain flexible and open to new possibilities.

We are most likely to succeed if we set goals that reflect who we are and tap into what we feel passionate about. It takes time, commitment and discipline to achieve goals that are challenging, so "we need to harness our energy and direct it toward what has the most meaning and value to us," writes Marti Olsen Laney.[10]

When I was 20 years old I set myself the goal of becoming a social worker. That meant that I first had to attend university in order to obtain a bachelor's degree. Typically it takes four years to complete a BSW, but it took me a lot longer because I had to pay for my own education and living expenses. Money was very tight. After I had completed the first two years of university I decided to take a year off to work full time so that I could afford to return to university and continue my education. Friends told me that I would never go back to school once I became used to a regular paycheque.

I did in fact return to my studies after taking that year off and I graduated from the University of British Columbia with a Bachelor of Social Work degree. This goal was a formidable one but I succeeded at achieving it. Why? Although I didn't know it at the time the goal fit with my life purpose and my values of learning and of helping people.

In retrospect, the link between my emotional energy and my success is clear. You too will find that when you tap into your life purpose and values and align them with your goals you'll have the energy to achieve them.

STOP & REFLECT

- IS THERE A CLEAR CONNECTION BETWEEN MY VALUES, MY LIFE PURPOSE, AND MY GOALS?
- IF NOT, WHAT CAN I DO TO CREATE THIS CONNECTION?

Personal development experts tell us that by setting goals we send a strong message to ourselves and to the universe that what we want is important. We can reinforce this by telling people in our support network about our plans and by asking them for their assistance. Most importantly, we have something to aim for so that we'll know when we have accomplished what we set out to do. In this way we can celebrate our achievements. Or, as so often happens, we do not achieve our goals, we can revise them. Perhaps the original goal needs to be broken down into smaller goals or the goal no longer fits with who we are or where we are going in life.

In any event, your goals must be your own and not ones that someone else has imposed upon you. You will find more detailed information about goal setting on the Mind Tools website.[11]

The key is not to get hung up on creating the perfect leadership development plan but to decide what is important for you, based on an overall vision of your life and the steps you'll need to take to get there. By creating a PLDP you will develop into a leader who is authentic, able to adapt to varying situations and circumstances, and confident about your abilities.

SELF-AWARENESS

To reach your potential you need to know yourself. Becoming self-aware can be challenging because we tend to see the world as we expect to see it and not necessarily as it really is. The same is true for how we see ourselves. We may get labelled at an early age. For instance, we may have been told that we are too quiet or not outgoing enough or we are not leadership material and we may end up believing these messages.

Recently I came across Patricia Cranton's *Personal Empowerment through Type* in my bookcase. I bought the book in 1998 while participating in the first annual Transformative Learning conference at Columbia University in New York. The book had lain dormant on my bookshelf for 14 years! When I opened it, an introductory comment by Cranton caught my eye: "Self-knowledge is the basis for personal empowerment."[12]

As Cranton writes, "To grow as individuals we must become aware of the tinted glasses through which we view the world".[13] In other words, we must examine the ways in which we are prevented from seeing the world as it is. Then we need to refocus. Sometimes we can learn to do this work ourselves and at other times we may need assistance from people who can help us see things more clearly.

What does self-knowledge mean to those of us who are introverts? Early on in my career I was asked to take on the leadership of a hospital program for elderly people with complicated medical problems. When my supervisor first broached the idea, I responded with an emphatic "no." I did not perceive myself as a leader and could not imagine my taking on the role that was being offered to me. This was not a case of wearing tinted or rose-coloured glasses—it was more like having blinders on. My supervisor did not give up on me. She suggested in no uncertain terms that the hospital needed me to take on the role of leader of the geriatric day hospital. After giving it some thought, I accepted the challenge.

In retrospect I can say that the four and one-half years that I spent in that position were some of the best years of my career in health care. Had I let my limiting beliefs about my abilities get the better of me, I would never have had that opportunity to grow as an individual. It was a great privilege to work with the outstanding team of health professionals who worked in the day hospital. I'm forever grateful for the people who saw leadership potential in me and pushed me out of my comfort zone.

In those days my leadership development plan existed only in my head. Although I was good at setting goals, I had not yet discovered the tools that I unearthed when I began to work as an organizational development consultant.

No matter where you are on your career path, a PLDP is an invaluable tool for your professional development. By creating and updating your PLDP on a regular basis your confidence in yourself will be boosted and you will learn to lead in a way that is authentic and unique.

AUTHENTICITY

Fifteen years ago, self-described introvert and university professor Patricia Cranton wrote, "Not knowing about our own personality...makes a person feel that there is something wrong if they don't have the same preference as others."[14]

For too long now introverts have been made to feel inferior for not being more extroverted. As introverts, it is not an easy thing to accept ourselves when the world tells us that we should be more social, outspoken, energetic, exciting, and charismatic. By learning more about what it means to be an introvert we can build on our strengths and be confident about who we are and what we have to offer the world.

Knowing who we are and acting with integrity are the hallmarks of authenticity. As we strive to fulfil our leadership potential or roles, we can always come back to this knowledge. As you become more self-aware you will naturally develop into an authentic leader, a person whose actions align with their values, who is honest, who people trust, respect and want to follow.

We can become more extroverted when we need to but we have to consciously develop this side of our personality in a way that honours who we are. Using a journal is an excellent tool to help us reflect as we move foreward.

JOURNALING

What is reflection? Reflection encourages us to look back on, think critically about, and learn from our experience. In short, it requires us to consciously stop what we are doing to pause and reflect.

Authors Daniel Goleman, Richard Boyatzis & Annie McKee have this to say about leaders unable to pause and reflect. "In the rush to achieve their goals and complete their tasks, they short themselves on learning to lead better."[15] As an introvert, you may have the advantage here because it is in your nature to pause and reflect and a journal is an excellent place to record your thoughts and feelings.

Journals have been used for years as a tool for professional development. I ask students to keep a journal as part of the requirements for a leadership course that I teach. The journal is a place for them to contemplate what they are learning and I ask them to share their enhanced knowledge with me at the end of the course.

Your journal can act as a "restorative niche" as it allows time for reflection and the synthesizing of new information and ideas. Writing in a journal can also provide you with a place to explore solitude.

A journal is a private place to record your thoughts, feelings, and experiences. I am never without a small notebook. Over the years I have found that if I don't write ideas down as they pop into my head, they are lost. Of course, my notebooks are also places that I jot down recipes, an interesting website or book or someone's name and phone number.

As you work through the questions in this chapter I recommend that you use a journal or create a place to write down your thoughts, ideas and questions. There are as many different journals as there are people using them. I continue to use a bound paper notebook, but today there are digital options such as using a smart phone or tablet to record your ideas or one of the many digital apps that are being developed to help us stay focused and on top of our lives.

There are no rules for journal writing and you are certainly not limited to writing. Many people like to doodle, draw pictures and add photos or cards. Here are some questions to get you started.

STOP AND REFLECT

- WHO AM I?
- HOW AM I UNIQUE?
- WHAT AM I MEANT TO DO WITH MY LIFE? WHAT IS MY LIFE'S PURPOSE?
- WHAT AM I PASSIONATE ABOUT?
- WHAT ARE MY VALUES? WHAT IS IMPORTANT TO ME?

- WHAT ARE SOME OF THE BIGGEST CHALLENGES THAT I'VE FACED IN MY LIFE? HOW DID I OVERCOME THEM?"
- WHAT ARE SOME OF THE CHALLENGES FACING ME NOW?
- WHAT ARE SOME UNUSUAL SKILLS THAT I HAVE?"
- WHAT AM I PROUD OF HAVING ACCOMPLISHED IN MY LIFE?
- WHAT DO PEOPLE TELL ME THAT I'M GOOD AT?
- WHAT CAN I DO BETTER THAN OTHER PEOPLE?
- WHAT DO OTHERS SEE AS MY STRENGTHS? (HINT, ASK THEM)

YOUR LEGACY

I had not thought about my legacy until I started teaching leadership classes. We all leave one whether or not we are aware of it. People often don't think about this concept when they are young. But one benefit of thinking about legacy at an early age is that it can help guide you as you move forward in your life. Take a moment and begin to think about the legacy that you would like to leave.

STOP & REFLECT

- WHAT DIFFERENCE DO I WANT TO MAKE?
- WHAT WILL BE MY GREATEST CONTRIBUTIONS?
- WHAT DO I WANT TO CREATE FOR MYSELF AND OTHERS?
- WHAT TYPE OF LEADER DO I WANT TO BE IN THREE YEARS? FIVE YEARS? TEN YEARS?
- WHAT IS MY DREAM?
- HOW WOULD I LIKE TO CHANGE THE WORLD?
- HOW DO I WANT TO BE REMEMBERED?
- IF I HAD UNLIMITED RESOURCES, WHAT WOULD I ACCOMPLISH?

Your legacy is how you will be remembered for the contributions you make and for the relationships that you develop with people. Although your legacy is what you leave behind after you die it is continually influenced throughout your life by your vision, goals, life purpose, values, and experiences and so becomes an important part of who you are as a leader. While completing your PLDP consider how you might create something lasting and beneficial.

While researching material for this section, I came across Dolly Garl's website[16] which is full of information and ideas to help you explore your legacy.

CHAPTER SUMMARY

- The benefits of being an introvert are increasingly being recognized and by working on your own development you will be poised to take advantage of leadership opportunities as the arise.

- Creating a Personal Leadership Development Plan (PLDP) is a great way to help you focus on the areas that you need to develop and to monitor your success as you achieve your goals.

- PLDPs typically include: vision, purpose, values, personality traits, individual strengths and areas for improvement, action plans, and thoughts about the legacy one wants to leave.

- Becoming self-aware is challenging but a necessary step in becoming a leader.

CHAPTER SEVEN
The Quiet Revolution Has Begun

"INTROVERTS OF THE WORLD, UNITE!"
Jonathan Rauch [1]

When I told my extroverted friend Barb that I was organizing a Meetup for introverts, she smiled and asked, "Will anyone show up?" When we both stopped laughing, I had to confess that I didn't know the answer to her question so I decided to do some investigating. What I discovered might surprise you. There is a Meetup for introverts in Toronto, Ontario. This group was founded in 2008 and currently lists 3773 members!

I have to admit that I was surprised by the sheer number of members and the fact that this Meetup was formed in 2008, four years before Susan Cain's popular book, *Quiet*, hit the New York Times best seller list. And, although the success of the Toronto Meetup came as a surprise, it shouldn't have. While researching and writing this book I discovered that introverts are quietly providing leadership in all sectors of our society, often without any recognition. These are people who have succeeded despite the barriers (self-imposed or otherwise) that they have managed to overcome. As dynamic introverts they have showed courage, resilience, and tenacity on the road to becoming leaders. At the same time many of them have had to hide their true natures in order to get ahead in the world.

Fortunately for all of us there is a growing interest in learning about what it means to be an introvert in the 21st century. The need to adopt a more introverted world view has been growing for some time, writes Nancy Okerlund. "Our extroverted culture is longing for more introvert energy—more quiet, more reflection, and a slower pace."[2]

There are signs that a quieter, more reflective society is gradually evolving. In our hectic world many of us are constantly seeking to find a balance in our lives. According to American work/life expert Vania Parakati, the understanding of this need for balance goes back centuries, but it was not until the 1980s that organizations began implementing policies to address this area of concern.[3]

Today, in our 24/7 world, I believe that the collective yearning for a more balanced approach to life and work is even stronger. This desire is reflected in many different ways in our society. Consider the ongoing challenge of finding a balance between:

- listening and talking

- work and our personal lives

- being alone and being with other people

- activity and rest

- introversion and extroversion

It almost seems as if there has been a game of tug of war between the personality traits of introversion and extroversion, with extroversion winning most of the games until now. But the world is different today and "we are poised on the brink of dramatic change,"[4] notes Susan Cain. I agree that we are in the midst of a sea change. A different kind of energy is emerging in the world.

In *The Tipping Point*, Malcolm Gladwell asks, "What can we do to deliberately start and control positive epidemics of our own?"[5] I like to think that Gladwell's positive epidemics are similar to quiet revolutions—periods of rapid social change that occur peacefully.

For introverts, this revolution is slow in coming but it is gaining traction. Over the past 10—12 years, individual writers have contributed to our current understanding of the mystery of what it means to be an introvert, how the introvert's mind works, and why, despite the fact that we make up 50% of the population, introverts are often overlooked and misunderstood.

In *Introvert Power*, Laurie Helgoe describes the process that she went through to document the percentage of introverts versus extroverts in the general population in North America. According to Helgoe, "we internalize the assumption that extroversion is normal and introversion is a deviation."[6] Her message is clear: be openly introverted and take back your power.

A PERFECT STORM

The storm has been building for some time. Initially it was more like a gentle onshore breeze but over the years it has gained power as the world embraced one new technology after another. Nowadays it seems that we are always connected. As a baby boomer I can remember a time before cell phones and computers when no one from work would consider phoning you at home after hours or on the weekends. Now we are expected to be on call all the time.

The term 24/7 was coined to describe the phenomenon of businesses being open or available 24 hours a day, seven days a week, and 365 days a year. The idea spread like wild fire as companies realized the potential financial gains. This dramatic change in how we live and work coincided with the rise of internet access and use. As more people began working 24/7, the more they began asking for and using services that were available around the clock. As a society we have, for the most part, accepted this accelerated rhythm of life.

But being on all the time is not without pitfalls. One consequence is that it has become increasing difficult to escape the noise, the activity, and of course the people. And, there are more dire consequences. "We are losing our listening," cautions sound expert Julian Treasure. "This is a serious problem as listening is our access to understanding and making meaning of what we hear."[7] Treasure suggests that people are more prone to conflict and violence when they feel that they haven't been listened to; he advocates that we spend some time each day in silence or at least being quiet for a few minutes.

There are other signs that the western world is ready for a quiet revolution.

Since the 1960s there has been a steady rise in interest in meditation and yoga. At first those seeking a quieter, more reflective lifestyle were seen as being outside the mainstream population. Now, the tide is changing as the benefits of turning inward are better known and documented through scientific research. Some progressive organizations even provide meditation rooms for employees to use.

As someone who embarked on meditation years ago, I support the efforts of these organizations. Ideally, every employee, regardless of whether he or she practises meditation, should have access to areas in the workplace that promote solitude and quiet reflection.

Another sign that we are in the midst of a quiet revolution is reflected in recent blog posts and articles linking stress, anxiety, and lack of productivity to that fact that we are connected at all times. In 2013 Fast Company published a series of blog posts aptly titled "Unplugged," providing examples of people who have had enough of being ruled by their electronic devices and who have found ways to disconnect themselves from the 24/7 world.[8]

John O'Ceallaigh, writing in *The Daily Telegraph*, provides examples of two unique approaches to helping people become 'unplugged': A "Silence Room" at Selfridge's store in London where shoppers can rest without the intrusion of cell phones and "No Wi-Fi benches" located in an area that blocks Wi-Fi signals in the City of Amsterdam.[9]

The ongoing research into the effects of multi-tasking on communication skills is another indicator of our growing awareness of the negative aspects of non-stop connectivity. The importance of working in environments free from interruptions was touched on in Chapter Three. Canadian academics Jane Webster and Ann-Frances Cameron have recently shed new light on the impact of interruptions on employee relationships.

Webster and Cameron studied the impact on communication in the workplace of multitasking using electronic devices. To describe this phenomenon they used the term multicommunicating or, as Wikipedia describes it "engaging in more than one conversation at a time."[10] They found, not surprisingly, that multicommunicating is often perceived as uncivilized behaviour in the workplace.

Not only is this form of communicating seen as discourteous but it also has a negative impact on trust and can undermine employee relationships. According to Jane Webster, "some people interpret it differently, and the ones that like to focus on one task get offended quite quickly. It's important to know how the people you work with like to communicate."[11] Throughout this book I've encouraged readers to speak up and tell their colleagues why they need periods of solitude in order to do their best thinking and their best work.

Not only does multitasking and multicommunicating affect our personal and work relationships; it also takes away from our ability to be creative and to solve problems.

But it doesn't have to be this way. Successful CEOs such as Warren Buffet, Bill Gates and Jeff Weiner all schedule regular blocks of time during the day so that they won't be interrupted. Weiner, CEO of LinkedIn, calls this time "free space" and P.M. Forin, author of *The Thinking Life*, refers to this time as "an investment".[12]

If I were to read between the lines of these articles and blog posts, I would hazard a guess that these quiet revolutionaries are in fact introverts. Introverts who are not afraid to spend time alone in quiet reflection. As introverts we need this time to sort and sift through what we are hearing, seeing and observing and, perhaps more importantly, to make sense of all that we are taking in.

Generally speaking we are not taught how to be solitary or how spending time alone can be advantageous, unless we are fortunate to have a teacher like Melanie.

At the beginning of the school year Melanie, who teaches high school English in Vancouver, shares with students the importance of creating a quiet space in which to think and write. But when she asks them what they can do to get into "the creativity zone" she finds that most of them haven't given it any thought.

> *"I encourage them to think of places they can go outside of home BUT I know that's not always an option (so many parents aren't comfortable with their teens being out of the home on a school night) so I also urge them to create a space in their bedrooms that is conducive to creativity....this is different for everyone but I remind them their phones and computers do actually turn off! (Ha ha)—they can put on music they find inspiring, light candles etc. but it is important to let their minds be quiet for a bit before they try to write."*[13]

And although she's not focusing specifically on introverts Melanie's approach creates a classroom climate that supports introverted students in their learning.

The signs that the world is ready for "more introverted energy" continue to emerge and the examples described in this chapter provide us with the ammunition we can use to advocate for the quiet time that we need. What started out looking like the perfect storm will, I hope, turn into a virtuous circle as increasing numbers of us begin to experience the positive benefits of turning off, slowing down, and spending time alone.

A CALL TO ACTION

At the beginning of this book we learned that introverts are as dynamic as extroverts and that by tapping into our passion and purpose in life we can make positive change happen. Change will only come when we discover that we have the power to influence the world around us both individually and collectively. As dynamic introverts, we no longer have to hide to get what we need; we can be a force for positive change by building on our quiet strengths.

There are numerous ways that we can do this. We can start by sharing information about introverts and introversion with our friends, family, and colleagues. This may not be as difficult as it sounds. I have often heard that "change occurs one conversation at a time," so the next time you are talking with someone, tell them that you're an introvert. You may be pleasantly surprised at where the conversation leads you.

I get very different reactions when I say I am writing a book about dynamic introverts. Extroverts are often amused by the idea that introverts can be dynamic. And when introverts first hear the words introvert and dynamic in the same sentence their first response is to shake their heads "no." After giving it some thought they frequently say "of course."

In the process of writing this book I also discovered that introverts are interested in learning more about introversion. They are keen to share their stories and to ask questions. Like me, many of them had never given much thought to this aspect of who they are.

Nick, a self-described introvert, told me a story about his cousin, a pilot in the United States Navy. A fellow introvert, modest about his abilities, Nick's cousin dreamt of becoming a strike fighter pilot. Most of the pilots who were competing with him for a training position were aggressive Type A personalities who saw themselves as the next generation of Tom Cruise but Nick's cousin was ultimately chosen because he was able to demonstrate that he was the best person for the job. He was recognized as such despite being modest about his abilities. The secret to his success: he remained true to himself. I believe that the moral of this story is "don't deny who you are in order to fit in."[14]

In the process of writing *The Dynamic Introvert* I heard many similar stories and I have come to believe that as introverts we have a need to share our experiences with people who we can relate to and who understand us. Fortunately this community of introverts is growing.

BUILDING COMMUNITY

A community of introverts is a place where we can connect and share our own stories.

What do I mean by building community? How is community created and how does being a part of a community benefit all of us? A community shares interests, concerns, hopes, beliefs and values. It provides us with an identity and a sense of belonging. A community can be geographical—think of the neighbourhood where you live. Or it can be virtual thanks to the reach of the internet.

The benefits of belonging to a community of like-minded people are numerous. It seems that for too long now many of us have felt isolated because of our introversion. Encouraged to act like extroverts, we often disregarded the core of our personalities—that which makes us unique. People I have talked to have spoken of feeling that there was something out of kilter but not knowing what. If you are feeling isolated and want to connect with other introverts you may have to create your own community.

One of the fastest growing social media sites is Meetup[15]. This site makes it easy for us to spend time with people who have similar interests. I believe that the site is growing rapidly in response to people's hunger for the experience of community. In fact the tag line on the home page of the website echoes this longing for a sense of community, "Meetups are neighbours getting together to learn something, do something, share something". There is even a Meetup in my area described as "networking for people who hate networking."

As we saw in Chapter Four, networking is an important skill for all leaders. As dynamic introverts we can be "super-connectors".[16] This is a term coined by Shane Snow, a New York City-based technology writer. Super-connectors focus on helping others achieve their goals. Dynamic introverts connect with people on-line and off-line. Although introverts may be more comfortable using social media such as LinkedIn, Facebook or Twitter, we are also excellent when it comes to communicating face-to-face. Step out of your office, join a group, speak up at a meeting, or take someone out for a cup of tea, coffee or a glass of wine.

Throughout this book I have shared examples of research on new models of leadership that highlight the benefits of a quieter, more reflective approach to influencing others. Here are some of the quiet strengths described by the introverted leaders whose stories appear in this book, They:

- Consider ideas before expressing an opinion
- Take time to prepare for important meetings
- Analyze information and situations
- Reflect before taking action
- Pay attention to detail
- Remain organized
- Act and react calmly

They are:

- Diplomatic
- Interested in what others have to say
- Thoughtful
- Comfortable with silence
- Observant
- Trustworthy
- Creative

I encourage you to add your own strengths to this list. Look at these often to remind yourself of who you are and what makes your leadership style extraordinary. Trust yourself and others will trust and follow you. The courage to find your voice—to speak with personal authority—will happen only when you become conscious of how your introversion is an asset. Taking back your power may feel risky but you will find strength in knowing that you are part of a growing community of dynamic introverts who are quietly providing leadership around the world.

By becoming a conscious introvert and by understanding what it means to be introverted we can gain a better understanding of who we are. Self-knowledge is one of the most important skills for all leaders and necessary if we are to reach our leadership potential. The more we know about introversion the less likely we will be confused by our own behaviour or send mixed signals to others.

My challenge to you is to share your story with others. Tell people you are an introvert, be a role model for someone younger, start a conversation, embrace your quiet strengths, and find the courage to step up and lead.

Finally, we can all be extraordinary leaders. We are all unique in what we can contribute. It is for this reason that Rosa Parks said, "Each person must live their life as a model for others."[17]

CHAPTER SUMMARY

- There is a growing interest in learning about introversion and a longing for a quieter more reflective world.

- Introverts can positively influence the world around them by explaining why they need quiet time in order to do their best work.

- Successful leaders in some of the world's largest organizations make it a priority to spend time in solitude.

- Becoming unplugged or taking time to detoxify from technology are trends that will make it easier for introverts to advocate for quiet time.

- Introverts are increasingly connecting with one another and this global community of support is growing.

AFTERWORD
Some Thoughts for Younger Generations

> "A HIGH SCHOOL STUDENT OF MINE WHO WAS
> AN EXCELLENT CANDIDATE FOR A DEMANDING SUMMER POSITION
> AT A HOSPITAL IS AN INTROVERT AND
> DOES NOT ALWAYS APPEAR ENTHUSIASTIC WHEN
> SHE MEETS SOMEONE NEW.
> ONCE YOU GET TO KNOW HER SHE IS WARM AND AN
> EXCELLENT CONVERSATIONALIST."
> Victoria[1]

What could this high student have done differently in order to ace the job interview? She might have identified herself as an introvert, which is not an easy thing to do especially when you are young and may lack self-confidence. Fortunately telling people that you are an introvert is becoming easier as more and more introverts speak up, but how many high school students know whether or not they are introverted or extroverted?

Becoming aware of one's preferences usually doesn't happen overnight. You may be fortunate to have a parent or a teacher who appreciates the challenges faced by introverts and is able to help you to understand and celebrate your unique personality. Typically an understanding of one's personality develops slowly, over time, and involves some form of personality testing. These types of tools may be not available to you until you enter college or the workforce.

I only discovered that I was an introvert when I completed the Myers Briggs Type Indicator (MBTI) at work as part of a team building exercise. I sometimes wonder if my life would have been different if I had learned about my personality traits in college or even earlier. Perhaps, but it may not have mattered as the world in the 1960s and 1970s was overwhelmingly geared toward extroverts.

Today, things are changing, thanks in part to the work of Marti Olsen Laney, Laurie Helgoe, Jennifer B. Kahnweiler, Judy Curson, Cassy Taylor, Adam S. McHugh, Nancy Ancowitz, Susan Cain, Trina M'Lot and others. Now, it seems that conversations about what it means to be an introvert are popping up everywhere in the media, on the internet and in our workplaces and our schools.

A few years ago I was invited to speak to a group of high school students. The teaching assistant[2] who contacted me requested that I "highlight the fact that introversion is a different way of being rather than something that one has to overcome" He felt that "the introverted students were continually treated and judged by standards [of extroversion] and as a result some introverts may not reach their full potential."[1] I applaud this young man for being proactive in recognizing the needs of introverted students but the fact that this was still happening in our schools saddenes me.

I am, however, excited about the possibilities opening up for introverts, especially for those who are still in school or just starting out in their careers. I am heartened by the example of an introverted 24-year-old university student from Vancouver Island. Trina M'Lot took advantage of her graduating project in graphic design to develop a both a project and a website,[3] part of which was directed toward young introverts. Trina's goal is "to encourage more students from elementary age to university to be more accepting of their modest natures."[4]

We are in the midst of a fundamental shift in how the world understands introverts. In future the students who are currently in the school system will benefit from these changes. They will no longer be expected to behave like extroverts and the traits that make them unique, e. g. the ability to listen and to stop and reflect will be regarded as highly as the extroverted traits of being outgoing, social, and charismatic.

I asked participants in my recent survey on introversion and leadership what advice they would give a young introvert starting out in his or her career. Here are some of their thoughts:

- Be yourself and believe in yourself. Discover the unique advantages that you bring to the "table" and learn all you can about your strengths. Learn to play to your strengths as an introvert. Self-acceptance is a great confidence builder.

- Take time to learn and understand what being an introvert means to you. Understand where it might limit you in your career, and use that insight to overcome these challenges.

- Find a mentor or a coach who will help you stay on track and accountable for your goals. Seek out someone who understands your personality type and work on building skills in areas where you are challenged.

- Take risks and push yourself out of your comfort zone. Tell people that you are an introvert and ask for what you need.

- Be authentic. There is a place for you to be exactly who you are! Don't overextend yourself by trying to be someone you're not.

- Learn about energy and your energy needs. Find ways to "recharge" when your batteries are low.

- Get to know other introverts, get their insights and learn from their experience. Connect with people who understand and who will support you. It will help if you are open about being an introvert.

- Follow your passion and use this to develop a personal leadership development plan to take into account your values and talents, etc. and what you want to accomplish.

- Recognize the challenges that you face and when you find yourself in a bad place, don't be tough, walk away. It's not worth it. There is a place for you to be exactly who you are.

- Be patient—don't expect things to change overnight!

- Know that there is nothing negative or wrong with being an introvert. Some people think it's a sign of weakness, when it is not. People need to hear that and hear the differences between an introvert and an extrovert, and know that neither one is better than the other.

- Celebrate who you are! It's cool to be an introvert!

Notes

INTRODUCTION

1. Judy Curson, email message to author, July 31 2013.
2. Jennifer B. Kahnweiler, *The Introverted Leader: Building on Your Quiet Strength* (San Francisco: Berrett-Koehler, 2009).

CHAPTER ONE

1. QUOTE BY JAMES BERNARD PRATT, JR.EMAIL MESSAGE TO AUTHOR, NOVEMBER 29, 2013. SEE ALSO HTTP://THEPRATDYNAMIC.WORDPRESS.COM/2013/09/20/110, ACCESSED ON NOVEMBER 29,2013
2. Beverly Alimo-Metcalfe and John Alban-Metcalfe, "Engaging Leadership: Creating organizations that maximize the potential of their people," Research Insight 4585 (The Chartered Institute of Personnel Development, September 2008)http://www.cipd.co.uk/shapingthefuture/_leadershipreport.htm,accessed on July 31, 2013.
3. Marty Olsen Laney, *The Introvert Advantage: How to Thrive in an Extroverted World* (New York: Workman, 2002).
4. Laurie Helgoe, "Revenge of the Introvert", *Psychology Today*, October, 2010, 54—61.
5. Ronald Reggio, post on "Why Can't Introverts Be Leaders?" posted on October 27, 2012, the Psychology Today blog http://www.psychologytoday.com/blog/cutting-edge-leadership/201210/why-can-t-introverts-be-leaders,accessed on Nov 6, 2013.
6. See, http://www.introvertedleaders.co.uk
7. Kirk Bizley, *Examining Physical Education for AQA* (Halley Court: Heinemann, 2001), 64.
8. Telephone interview with Dr. Judy Curson. Judy Curson developed the website, http://www.introvertedleaders.co.uk with Cassy Taylor.

9. David Rock, post on "Leadership on the Brain", the Harvard Business Review Blog, posted on April 28, 2010, http://www.blogs.hbr.org, accessed on October 2013.

10. See, http://en.wikipedia.org/wiki/Leadership_studies

11. James M. Kouzes and Barry Z. Posner, *The Leadership Challenge* (San Francisco: Jossey-Bass, 2007), 23.

12. Adam M. Grant, Fransesca Gino, and David A. Hofman, "The Hidden Advantages of Quiet Bosses,"*Harvard Business Review*, December, 2010, http://hbr.org/2010/12/the-hidden-advantages-of-quiet-bosses/ar/1, accessed in October 2013.

13. Joann Lublin, post "Introverted Execs Find Ways to Shine" posted on *Wall Street Journal*, April 14, 2011, http://online.wsj.com/news/articles/SB10001424052748703983104576263053775879800, accessed on November 5, 2013.

14. Adam S. McHugh, *Introverts in the Church: Finding Our Place in an Extroverted Culture* (Downers Grove: Intervarsity Press, 2009), 114.

15. As quoted in Susan Cain, *Quiet: The Power of Introverts in a World That Can't Stop Talking* (New York: Crown, 2012), 51.

16. Jonathan Rauch post "Caring for Your Introvert" posted on *The Atlantic*, March 1, 2003, http://www.theatlantic.com/magazine/archive/2003/03/caring-for-your-introvert/302696/, (accessed on November 10, 2013)

17. Kahnweiler, *The Introverted Leader*, 4.

18. This famous quote by Sir Winston Churchill former British prime minister can be found in numerous places. This one is from the website http://www.quotationspage.com/quotes/Sir_Winston_Churchill/21

19. Brené Brown, *Daring Greatly: How the Courage to be Vulnerable Transforms the Way We Live, Love, Parent, 1and Lead (New York: Penguin, 2012)*, 2.

20. See, http://www.introvertenergy.com/freestuff.php for information about conscious introverts.

21. Tom Peters, "The Brand Called You", *Fast Company*(August,1997), available online http://www.fastcompany.com/28905/brand-called-you,accessed on June 29, 2013.

22. Daniel Goleman, Richard Boyatzis and Annie McKee, *Primal Leadership: Learning to Lead with Emotional Intelligence* (Boston: Harvard Business School Press, 2004), 45.

23. See, for example http://berkana.org/ for more on the writing of Margaret Wheatly.
24. A definition of shyness can be found on the Shyness Research Institute at Indiana University Southeast website, see http://www.ius.edu/shyness
25. Elaine Aaron, post on "Understanding the Highly Sensitive Person: Sensitive, Introverted, or Both?" *Psychology Today*, posted on July 21, 2011, http://www.psychologytoday.com/blog/attending-the-undervalued-self/201107/understanding-the-highly-sensitivity-person-sensitive-int, accessed on October 28, 2013.
26. Elaine Aron, *The Highly Sensitive Person* (New York: Broadway Books Group, 1996).
27. See also http://www.hsperson.com for a Dr. Aaron's self-test on sensitivity.
28. Brian R. Little, post on "Acting Out of Character in the Immortal Profession: Toward a Free Trait Agreement," *Academicmatters* posted in April, 2010 http://www.academicmatters.ca/2010/04/acting-out-of-character-in-the-immortal-profession-toward-a-free-trait-agreement/, accessed in November, 2013.

CHAPTER TWO

1. Susan Krauss Whitbourne, post on "Why Introverts Make Great Leaders—Sometimes," the Psychology Today blog, posted on November 8, 2011 http://www.psychologytoday.com/blog/fulfillment-any-age/201111/why-introverts-make-great-leaders-sometimes, accessed in September, 2012.
2. Adam M. Grant, Francesca Gino and David A. Hofmann, Reversing the Extraverted Leadership Advantage: The Role of Employee Proactivity," *Academy of Management Journal*, Vol. 54, No. 3 (2011):528-550
3. The Facts of Life television series ran from 1979—1988 in the United States. See http://www.imdb.com/title/tt0078610/ .
4. See also http://www.leadershipchallenge.com for information about current research, events, services and resources.
5. David Rock, *Quiet Leadership: Six Steps to Transforming Performance at Work* (New York: HarperCollins, 2006).
6. Dan McCarthy, post on "Most New Managers are Clueless About What it Takes to be Successful," the Great Leadership by Dan blog, posted on March 4, 2011. http://www.greatleadershipbydan.com/2011/03/most-new-managers-are-clueless-about.html, accessed in October 2012).

7. Neal Burgis, post on "Successful Introverted CEOs," the Business Expert Seminars blog, posted on nd http://www.businessexpertwebinars.com/content/view/369/29, accessed in October, 2013).

8. Leo Babauta, post on "Finding Your Voice," the Zen Habits blog, posted on July 23, 2011. http://zenhabits.net/voice/, accessed in October, 2013.

9. See http://www.toastmasters.org for information on clubs in your area, the history of toastmasters, resources for public speaking and leadership development.

10. Jim Collins, *Good to Great: Why Some Companies Make the Leap and Others Don't* (New York: HarperCollins: 2001), 13.

11. Cain, *Quiet*,1.

12. David R. Hawkins, *Power vs Force: The Hidden Determinants of Human Behavior* (Carlsbad: Hay House, 2002), 183.

13. Ralph H. Kilmann, email message to author, April 4, 2013.

14. Kilman Diagnostics website,http://www.kilmanndiagnostics.com

15. Conflict Resolution Network website, http://www.crnhq.org

16. Joseph A. Raelin, "I Don't Have Time to Think! Versus the Art of Reflective Practice," *Reflections*, Vol. 4, No1 (2002): 66-79.

17. Peter Senge, *The Fifth Discipline: The Art and Practice of the Learning Organization* (New York: Doubleday, 1994).

18. See also the website for the Society for Organizational Learning, http://www.solonline.org

19. The term personal mastery is one of five disciplines described in *The Fifth Discipline*. The other four are: systems thinking, mental models, building shared vision, and team learning.

CHAPTER THREE

1. Mira Kirshenbaum, *The Emotional Energy Factor: The Secrets High-Energy People Use to Beat Emotional Fatigue* (New York:Bantam Dell,2004), 2.

2. In Chapter Three of her book *The Introvert Advantage*, author Marti Olsen Laney provides a thorough description of how an introvert's brain functions, 61-94.

3. Heike Bruch, Brend Vogel and Felicitas Morhart, "Keeping Track of Organizational Energy: How to Harness a Company's Productive Forces," *CriticalEYE* June—August (2005): 65-71.

4. Kirshenbaum, *The Emotional Energy Factor*, 4.

5. Jim Loehr and Tony Swartz, *The Power of Full Engagement: Managing Energy, Not Time, Is the Key to High Performance and Personal Renewal* (New York: The Free Press, 2005).
6. Laney, The Introvert Advantage, 258.
7. Tina Coleman, post on "Solitude: Alone, but Not Lonely" Beliefnet posted on November 2011 http://www.beliefnet.com/healthandhealing/getcontent.aspx?cid=14233,accessed in October 2013.
8. Goleman, Boyatzis & McKee, *Primal Leadership*, 8.
9. Ester Buchholz, post on "The Call of Solitude," Psychology Today posted on January, 1998 and reviewed on January, 2012 http://www.psychologytoday.com/articles/199802/the-call-solitude, accessed inNovember 2013.
10. Loehr and Swartz, 2003, 5.
11. Brian R. Little, post on "Acting Out of Character in the Immortal Profession: Toward a Free Trait Agreement," *Academicmatters* posted in April, 2010 http://www.academicmatters.ca/2010/04/acting-out-of-character-in-the-immortal-profession-toward-a-free-trait-agreement/, accessed in November, 2013.
12. For more information about the term "restorative niche", see B.R. Little, "Acting Out of Character in the Immortal Profession: Toward a Free Trait Agreement," *Academic Matters*, April-May, 2010,*available online- http://www.academicmatters.ca/2010/04/acting-out-of-*character-in-the-immortal-profession-toward-a-free-trait-agreement/; accessed on November 2, 2013.
13. Cain, *Quiet*, 84.
14. Richard.J. Leider, *The Power of Purpose: Creating Meaning in Your Life and Work* (San Francisco: Berrett-Koehler, 1997), 1.
15. Leider, *The Power of Purpose*, 1
16. Go to http://www.christianity.com/church/church-life/introvert-no-apology-required-11626582.html?p=0 to see editor Alex Crain's interview with Adam McHugh,author of *Introverts in the Church*.
17. Margarita Tartakovsky post on "Five Ways to Prevent Job Burnout," PsychCentral posted on April 30, 2012 http://psychcentral.com/blog/archives/2012/04/30/5-ways-to-prevent-job-burnout/, accessed in November 2013.
18. Sherrie B. Carter post on "How Superachievers Can Avoid Burnout," PsychologyToday posted on May 6, 2012 http://www.psychologytoday.com/blog/high-octane-women/201205/where-do-you-fall-the-burnout-continuum, accessed in November 2013.

19. Christina Maslach and Michael. P. Leiter, "Early Predictors of Job Burnout and Engagement," *Journal of Applied Psychology*, Vol. 93, No. 3 (2008):498-512.
20. Stephané Côté and Brian.R. Golden, "Emotional Intelligence and Burnout Among Leaders" (paper presented at the annual meeting for the Academy of Management, Atlanta, Georgia, August, 2006).
21. Laney, *The Introvert Advantage*, 11.
22. See http://www.secretan.com/tools/assessment-tools/job-burnout-survey
23. See http://www.kilmann.com
24. See http://www.mindtools.com for a number of resources on how to deal with burnout.

CHAPTER FOUR

1. Robin Fisher Roffer, *Make a Name for Yourself: 8 Steps Every Woman Needs to Create a Personal Brand Strategy for Success* (New York: Broadway Books, 2000), 2.
2. Laney, *The Introvert Advantage*, 5.
3. See http://www.mindtools.com
4. Roffer, *Make a Name for Yourself*, 13.
5. Tom Peters, post *The Brand Called You* posted on August 31, 1997 on the Fast Company blog,http://www.fastcompany.com/28905/brand-called-you,accessed on June 29, 2013.
6. Karley Cunningham. "How to Hire the Right Branding Agency," *Business in Vancouver*, July 3-9, 2012, 28.
7. Patsy Rodenburg, *The Second Circle: How to Use Positive Energy for Success in Every Situation* (New York: W.W. Norton & Company, 2008).
8. Rodenburg, *The Second Circle*, 10.
9. Ken Keis posted Source: Talent Smart, cited in CRG-Self Awareness: The Key to Transformation Issue 144 ISSN 1712-468,(accessed November 1, 2013)http://www.crgleader.com/ezine/livingonpurpose/LOP144.html
10. Roffer, *Make a Name for Yourself*, 167.
11. Susan Roane, *The Secrets of Savvy Networking* (New York: Warner Books,1993), 2.

12. Chelsea Emery. "Want a Better Job? Find yourself a mentor," *The Vancouver Sun*, September 15, 2012, C 6.
13. See http://www.peer.ca
14. Cheryl Richardson, *Stand Up for Your Life: Develop the Courage Confidence, and Character to Fulfill Your Greatest Potential* (New York: The Free Press, 2002).

CHAPTER FIVE

1. Mike Johnson, Career Development Consultant, email to author, November 28, 2012.
2. Collins, *Good to Great*, 41.
3. See http://en.wikipedia.org/wiki/The_war_for_talent for a detailed description of the term "war for talent".
4. Rodney Warrenfeltz, post on "Hiring Practices That Improve Employee Quality and Reduce Turnover" posted on the Performance Programs blog http://www.performanceprograms.com/surveys/Hiring_Practices_Improve_Quality_Reduce_Turnover.html, accessed on November 4, 2013.
5. Adam Grant, email to author, November 29, 2012.
6. Carmine Gallo post on "70% of Your Employees Hate Their Jobs" posted on November 11, 2011 on the Forbes blog http://www.forbes.com/sites/carminegallo/2011/11/11/your-emotionally-disconnected-employees/ , accessed on November 2, 2013.
7. Andy Johnson post on "Four Reasons CEOs Should Understand Introversion" posted on Price Associates blog http://www.price-associates.com/blog/Andy-Johnson/post/4-reasons-ceos-should-understand-introversion/ , assessed on July 2, 2015.
8. Patricia Cranton, *Personal Empowerment Through Type* (Sneedville: Psychological Type Press, 1998), 42.
9. Vanessa*, email to author, November 21, 2012. *Name changed to protect privacy.
10. Carol S. Dweck, *Mindset: The New Psychology of Success (New York: Ballentine Books, 2006).*
11. See http://ctb.ku.edu/en/table-of-contents/leadership/leadership-ideas/plan-for-building-leadership/main, accessed on November 2, 2013. The Community Toolbox is a public service of The University of Kansas and is a part of the KU Work Group's role as a designated World Health Organization Collaborating Centre for Community Health and Development.

12. Brent Richter, "Faith in Employees Gives Aerospace CEO Wings", *Business in Vancouver*, November 6, 2012. Accessed November 1, 2013. Story URL: http://www.biv.com/article/20121106/BIV020901/311069973/-1/BIV/faith-in-employees-gives-aerospace-ceo-wings
13. See http://www.vancity.com Click on the Careers tab for information about job interviews.
14. Rosalie Boulter, email to author, November 11, 2012.
15. Stacy Doepner, email to author, November 19, 2012.
16. Tom Peters and Robert Waterman, *In Search of* Excellence (New York: Harper & Row, 1982).
17. See http://hrcouncil.ca/home.cfm for information about performance reviews and other human resource practices.
18. Michael Haberman post "Are We Making a Mistake With Teamwork and Leadership?" posted on Omega HR Solutions on August 20, 2012 http://omegahrsolutions.com/2012/08/are-we-making-a-mistake-with-teamwork-and-leadership.html ,accessed on November 2, 2013.
19. See http://www.analytictech.com/mb021/teamhint.htm In the Manual for Working with Teams author Steve Borgatti shares his thoughts about working with introverted team members. Accessed on November 4, 2013.
20. See http://www.mindtools.com
21. Gillian Livingston post "Work a Source of Anxiety for Many Canadians" posted on The Globe & Mail May 14, 2013 http://www.theglobeandmail.com/report-on-business/careers/career-advice/life-at-work/work-a-source-of-anxiety-for-many-canadians/article11918348/ accessed on November 5, 2013.
22. See http://www.mindtools.com for information about burnout.

CHAPTER SIX

1. Joann S. Lublin post on "Introverted Execs Find Ways to Shine" posted on April 14 2011 on The Wall Street Journal http://online.wsj.com/news/articles/SB10001424052748703983104576263053775879800,- accessed on November 5, 2013.
2. Bill George, *Authentic Leadership: Rediscovering the Secrets to Creating Lasting Value* (San Francisco: Jossey-Bass, 2003).
3. Kouzes & Posner, *The Leadership Challenge*, 169.

4. Goleman, Boyatzis & McKee, *Primal Leadership*, 148.
5. Rhonda Byrne, *The Secret* (New York: Atria Books, 2006), 89.
6. Cranton, *Personal Empowerment through Type*, 11, 12.
7. For more information on situational leadership theory see http://www.kenblanchard.com/Solutions/Situational-Leadership-Development/Situational-Leadership-II and http://www.mindtools.com/pages/article/newLDR_44.htm
8. Cranton, *Personal Empowerment through Type*, 23.
9. See, http://www.mindtools.com for a variety of tools to assist with employee feedback and evaluation. The terms feedback and evaluation are used interchangeably in this chapter.
10. Laney, *The Introvert Advantage*, 231.
11. See, http://www.mindtools.com
12. Cranton, *Personal Empowerment through Type*, viii.
13. Cranton, *Personal Empowerment through Type*, 70.
14. Cranton, *Personal Empowerment through Type*, 89.
15. Goleman, Boyatzis & McKee, *Primal Leadership*, 157.
16. See, http://www.creatinglegacy.com

CHAPTER SEVEN

1. Stage Stossel posted "Introverts of the World Unite" posted on February 14, 2006 on The Atlantic http://www.theatlantic.com/magazine/archive/2006/02/introverts-of-the-world-unite/304646/, accessed on November 11, 2013.
2. Nancy Okerlund, on "This is the Time for Introverts", posted on December 11, 2008 on *Introverted En*ergy http://www.introvertenergy.com/introvertenergizer/introvertenergizer-02-19.php, accessed on November 10, 2013.
3. Vania Parakati post on "The History of Work/Life Balance: It's Not as New As You Think", posted September 30, 2010 on Examiner http://www.examiner.com/article/the-history-of-work-life-balance-it-s-not-as-new-as-you-think-1, accessed on September 20, 2013.
4. See http://www.ted.com/talks/susan_cain_the_power_of_introverts.html for Cain's discussion on how introverts are changing the world.

5. Malcolm Gladwell, *The Tipping Point* (New York: Little Brown & Company, 2002), 14.

6. Laurie Helgoe, *Introvert Power: Why Your Inner Life is Your Hidden Strength* (Naperville: Sourcebooks, 2008), 43.

7. See http://www.ted.com/talks/julian_treasure_5_ways_to_listen_better.html

8. See http://www.fastcompany.com/3012521/unplug/baratunde-thurston-leaves-the-internet to read the chronicle of author Baratunde Thurston's 25 days without the internet.

9. John O'Ceallaigh post on "Digital Detox Holidays: Switching off from technology dependency" posted on March 11, 201on The Telegraph http://www.telegraph.co.uk/luxury/travel/3317/digital-detox-holidays-switching-off-from-technology-dependency.html, accessed on October 25, 2013.

10. See http://en.wikipedia.org/wiki/Multicommunicating

11. Leah Eichler post on "Sorry to be rude but my smartphone needs my attention" posted on October 14, 2013 on The Globe and Mail http://www.theglobeandmail.com/report-on-business/careers/career-advice/life-at-work/sorry-to-be-rude-but-my-phone-needs-me/article14706158/, accessed onNovember 10, 2013.

12. P. M. Forni, *The Thinking Life* (New York: St. Martin's Griffin, 2011), 27.

13. Melanie*, email to author March 17, 2015. *Name changed to protect privacy.

14. Nick shared this story in a personal communication. He had asked me about the title of my book and when I told him, he asked if he could tell me a story about his cousin. I share Nick's story here to demonstrate the type of response that I received as I was researching and writing *The Dynamic Introvert*.

15. See http://www.meetup.com/ for information Meetup and how to organize a Meetup group.

16. Shane Snow post on "The Rise of the Superconnector" posted on April 2, 2013 on Fast Company http://www.fastcompany.com/3007657/rise-superconnector. accessed on November 10, 2013.

17. This famous quote by civil rights activist Rosa Parks can be found in numerous places. This version is from the website http://www.goodreads.com/quotes/128784-each-person-must-live-their-life-as-a-model-for, accessed November 11, 2013.

AFTERWORD

1. Victoria, email to author May 2, 2015. *Name changed to protect privacy.
2. Name omitted to protect privacy.
3. Erin Anderssen post on "When is Shyness an Illness?" posted on January 30, 2013 on The Globe and Mail http://www.theglobeandmail.com/life/health-and-fitness/health/when-is-shyness-an-illness/article8018705/, accessed on October 21, 2013.
4. See, http://www.greatmindsthinkdifferently.ca for information about Trina M'Lot's website.

Index

Symbols

360 degree evaluation 114

A

Accommodating introverts 97
Advocates for alone time 60
Aron, Elaine
   The Highly Sensitive Person 10, 144
Assertiveness 98, 149, 157
Authentic 8, 19, 28, 56, 69, 77, 118, 120, 121, 140
Authenticity 8, 73, 121
Awareness and education 89, 90

B

Bakken, Elizabeth
   Mindtools website 67
Balance 7, 48, 54, 68, 76, 77, 94, 126, 150
Borgatti, Steve
   Manual for Working with Teams 100
Boulter, Rosalie
   Relationship Coach 96, 149
Brain locking
   Marty Olsen Laney 66
Brown, Brené
   University of Houston 7
Buchholz, Ester 53, 146
Burnout 6, 62, 63, 64, 65, 66, 67, 106, 146, 147

C

Cain, Susan
   Quiet 5, 8, 36, 59, 125, 127, 138, 143
Call to action 131
Challenges Facing Introverts 5, 9, 21, 28, 29, 31, 40, 44, 46, 48, 56, 60, 81, 92, 100, 104, 123, 139, 140
Charisma 4, 77, 106
Chartered Institute of Personnel & Development
   Engaging Leadership 2
Churchill, Sir Winston
   British Prime Minister 7, 143
Coaching
   Leadership skill 11, 26, 27, 41, 67, 98, 104
Coaching conversations 26
Collins, Jim
   Good to Great 35, 44, 84, 145
Communication styles 87
Community of introverts 133
Conflict 34, 38, 39, 44, 56, 60, 62, 67, 89, 102, 114, 116, 128
Conflict Resolution Network 39, 145

Côté, Stéphane
  University of Toronto Rotman School of Management 64
Courage 7, 12, 17, 21, 24, 125, 135, 136
Cranton, Patricia
  Personal Empowerment through Type 90, 113, 119, 120, 148
Cunningham, Karley
  Business in Vancouver 75
Curson, Judy 3, 138, 142

D

Dialogue
  Listening 41, 90
Diversity 44, 88, 89, 91, 94
Diversity programs 88, 89
Doepner, Stacy
  University of Minnesota Human Resources 97, 149
Dweck, Carol
  Mindset 92

E

Emery, Chelsea 81
Emotional intelligence 9, 64, 65, 66, 68, 114
Employee engagement 86, 89, 97
Enabling others
  Leadership skill 23, 26
Energy
  Understanding necessary for dynamic introverts 21, 22, 27, 37, 44, 45, 46, 47, 48, 49, 50, 51, 53, 54, 55, 60, 61, 62, 65, 67, 68, 76, 77, 86, 106, 111, 115, 116, 117, 118, 126, 127, 131, 140

F

Fast Company
  Blog posts 129
Finding our voice 32
Formal leadership xiii
Freudenberger, Herbert J.
  Psychoanalyst 62

G

Gallup
  Employee engagement study 86
Garl, Dolly
  Legacy 124
George, Bill
  Authentic Leadership 109
Gino, Francesca 13, 44, 144
Gladwell, Malcolm
  The Tipping Point 127
Golden, Brian
  University of Toronto Rotman School of Management 64
Goleman, Daniel
  Emotional intelligence 5, 9, 110, 143
Google 4, 97
Grant, Adam
  Wharton School of Business 4, 13, 44, 85, 86, 108, 148
Group techniques
  Talking stick, ground rules, brainstorming 101

H

Haberman, Michael
  Omega HR Solutions 99
Hawkins, David
  Power vs Force 37

Helgoe, Laurie
   Introvert Power 127, 138, 142, 151
Hiring practices 95
Hofmann, David 13, 44
Human resources policies and procedures 94

I

Informal leadership xiii
Introspection 9, 19, 76
Introverted brand 12
Introverted leaders 3, 4, 11, 33, 36, 37, 53, 56, 85, 86, 134
Introverted managers
   And emotional intelligence 65
Introverted personality traits
   And leadership 14
Introverts
   Burnout and fairness 64
Invisible
   Hiding in plain sight 47, 56, 88

J

Job interviews 95
Journal writing
   Tool for self reflection 122
Jung, Carl vii, 90

K

Kahnweiler, Jennifer xiii, 6
Kilmann, Ralph H.
   Thomas-Kilman Conflict Mode Instrument 38, 145
Kirshenbaum, Mira
   The Emotional Energy Factor 45, 47, 145

Kouzes, James M.
   The Leadership Challenge 4, 23, 143

L

Laney, Marty Olsen
   The Introvert Advantage 2, 66, 142
Leadership development 11, 19, 94, 110, 114, 118, 120, 140
Learning Organizations xv, 41
Legacy 29, 123, 124
Leider, Richard J.
   The Power of Purpose 60, 61
Leiter, Michael
   Acadia University 64
Life purpose 44, 60, 61, 111, 117, 118, 124
Listening 7, 14, 40, 41, 43, 67, 72, 77, 101, 102, 126, 128
Little, Brian
   Pseudo extroversion 10, 57
Livingston, Sally 78
Loehr, Jim
   The Power of Full Engagement 48, 60, 146

M

Maslach, Christina
   University of California 64, 147
McCarthy, Dan 29, 144
McHugh, Adam
   Introverts in the Church 5, 62
Meditation and yoga 128
Meetup 133
Mentor 81, 82, 103, 140, 148

Mills, Daniel Quinn
  Harvard Business School 5
M'Lot, Trina
  Advocate for young introverts 138
Multi-tasking xi, 129
Myers Briggs Type Indicator 90, 138

N

Negative traits
  Associated with introversion 83
Networking 60, 74, 78, 79, 134

O

O'Ceallaigh, John
  The Daily Telegraph 129
Ohio State University
  Studies on the behaviour of leaders 4
Okerlund, Nancy
  Conscious introverts 8, 126, 150
Onboarding 94, 97, 104, 106
Open plan offices 59
Organizational Energy 54, 145

P

Parakati, Vania
  Worklife balance 126
Parks, Rosa
  Civil rights leader 37, 136, 151
Peer Resources
  Canadian Online Mentoring Company 81
Performance reviews 97, 98

Personal branding
  Leadership skill 6, 11, 69, 74, 82, 114
Personal energy 11, 47, 48, 52, 62, 66, 67, 111
Personality assessments 110
Personal leadership development plan PLDP
  PLDP 11, 19, 110, 140
Personal mastery
  Peter Senge 43, 145
Personal power 37, 76
Personal support network
  Preventing burnout 67
Personal SWOT
  Strengths, weaknesses, opportunities & threats 116
Peters, Tom 98, 149, 157
  The Brand Called You 8, 74, 98, 143, 147, 149
Posner, Barry Z.
  The Leadership Challenge 4, 23, 143
Pseudo extrovert 55
Public speaking x, 33, 34, 60, 78, 145

Q

Question the status quo
  Leadership skill 25
Quiet leaders
  Level five leadership 36
Quiet power 11, 36, 44
Quiet revolution 11, 128, 129
Quiet space 18, 22, 97

R

Rauch, Jonathan
  The Atlantic 5, 125, 143
Recognition 11, 17, 27, 28, 125
Recruitment 94, 106
Reflection 9, 40, 41, 51, 52, 54, 57, 76, 101, 102, 121, 122, 126, 129, 130
Resilience 21, 106, 114, 125
Respect 19, 56, 98, 101, 121
Respite 22, 51, 52, 54, 55, 67
Restorative niche
  Brian Little 57, 122, 146
Richardson, Cheryl
  Stand Up for Your Life 82
Rock, David
  Quiet Leadership 4, 26, 143, 144
Rodenburg, Patsy
  The Second Circle 76, 147
Roffer, Robin Fisher 69, 73, 77, 147, 157
Role models 16
Ruminating 82

S

Schellenberg, David
  Business in Vancouver 93
Secretan, Lance
  Burnout quiz 66
Self-awareness
  Leadership skill 9, 41, 55, 114
Self-confidence 8, 21, 30
Self-management
  Leadership skill 9, 41, 65
Senge, Peter
  The Fifth Discipline 41, 43, 145
Setting goals 117
Shared vision
  Leadership skill 23, 25

Situational leadership 113
Snow, Shane
  Super connectors 134

Solitude 9, 51, 53, 68, 102, 122, 129, 130, 136, 146
Stereotypes 90, 91
Stress, anxiety, and depression 105
Supportive environments
  Learning organizations 41
Swartze, Tony
  The Power of Full Engagement 60

T

Taylor, Cassy 3, 138, 142
Team building 90, 94, 138
The Leadership Challenge
  Leadership practices 4, 23, 109, 143, 149
The Shyness Research Institute
  Indiana University Southeast 10
The Six Rs
  Role models, recognition, resilience, resources, respect, respite 15
Thomas, Kenneth W.
  Thomas-Kilman Conflict Mode Instrument 38
Toastmasters International
  Leadership and public speaking 33
Treasure, Julian
  Sound expert 128

V

Values 115
Vision board 111
Vulnerability and leadership 7

W

War for talent
  Steven Hankin, McKinsey & Company 85
Warrenfeltz, Rodney
  Personality tests 85
Waterman, Robert 98, 149, 157
Whelchel, Lisa
  Introverted actor 16
Winning environments
  Ideal environments 59

Y

Young introverts 11

About the Author

Lesley was born in Lancashire, England and grew up on the West Coast of Canada. As a child she was quiet and reserved, an early indication of her introverted nature, but things began to change shortly after she left school. Soon after she graduated from high school she replied to an advertisement in the local newspaper. The ad was from the Crisis Centre in search of volunteers to help people in distress.

Summoning up her courage Lesley applied for and was interviewed for a volunteer position but was initially told that she was not a suitable candidate, perhaps because she was too quiet? Not long after the interview she was surprised to receive a call from the Crisis Centre inviting her to attend a series of training sessions. This early experience with helping other people led to a long and fulfilling career as a social worker, educator, and coach.

Over the years, Lesley has developed and taught leadership courses in the health care and not-for-profit sectors and in higher education. Today she continues to provide leadership coaching and training to individuals and teams. Lesley has a passion for writing and she has been a blogger and a newspaper columnist. She is a member of The Federation of B.C. Writers, The International Leadership Association (ILA), The International Coach Federation (ICF) and Toastmasters International.

www.ingramcontent.com/pod-product-compliance
Lightning Source LLC
Chambersburg PA
CBHW060525090426
42735CB00011B/2375